HE CAME DOWN FROM HEAVEN

HE CAME DOWN FROM HEAVEN

with which is reprinted
THE FORGIVENESS OF SINS

by Charles Williams

the apocryphile press
BERKELEY, CA
www.apocryphile.org

apocryphile press
BERKELEY, CA

Apocryphile Press
1700 Shattuck Ave #81
Berkeley, CA 94709
www.apocryphile.org

He Came Down from Heaven first published by Heinemann in
1938. *The Forgiveness of Sins* first published by G. Bles. in 1942.
First Apocryphile edition, 2005.

For sale in the USA only. Sales prohibited in the UK.
Printed in the United States of America.

ISBN 0-9764025-6-4

Contents

HE CAME DOWN FROM HEAVEN

THE FORGIVENESS OF SINS

HE CAME DOWN FROM HEAVEN

To
MICHAL
by whom I began to study
the doctrine of glory

CHAPTER I

Heaven and the Bible

The word Heaven occurs in the Lord's Prayer twice and in the Nicene Creed three times. The clauses which contain it are: 'Our Father which art in heaven'; 'Thy will be done on earth as it is in heaven'; 'Maker of heaven and earth'; 'Who for us men and for our salvation came down from heaven'; 'He ascended into heaven'. A single sentence, recurrent in the Gospels, is as familiar as these: 'The kingdom of heaven is at hand', or more briefly, 'The kingdom of heaven'.

The Oxford English Dictionary gives various definitions of the word. It is derived from the old English *hefen*. Its earliest meaning is the sky or firmament, the space above the world. It was applied afterwards to the various concentric circles into which that space was supposed to be divided, and presently to the same space considered as 'the habitation of God and his angels'. Hence, as early as Chaucer, it came to mean a state of spiritual being equivalent to the habitation of divine things, a state of bliss consonant with union with God. Its common meaning to-day, as a religious term, sways between the spiritual and the spatial, with the stress in general slightly, though unintentionally, more upon the second than the first.

This placing of the stress is no doubt due chiefly to the first clause of the Lord's Prayer. That Prayer is more widely known than any of the Creeds, and more habitually used than the phrase from the Gospels. Its opening words undoubtedly imply a place in which 'Our Father' exists, a spatial locality inhabited by God. Against this continual suggestion so easily insinuated into minds already too much disposed to it, the great theological definitions of God which forbid men to attribute to him any nature inhabiting place are less frequently found and less effectively imagined. They have to be remembered. But 'which art in heaven' is already remembered. Its easy implications have to be refused by attention.

It is not, of course, possible to deny that heaven—in the sense of salvation, bliss, or the presence of God—can exist in space; that would be to deny the Incarnation. But heaven, as such, only exists because of the nature of God, and to his existence alone all bliss is related. In a Jewish tradition God was called 'the Place' because all places were referred to him, but he not to any place. With this in mind it might be well that private meditation should sometimes vary the original clause by 'Our Father in whom is heaven'. The change is for discipline of the mind, for though it is incapable of the apparent superficiality yet it is also incapable of the greater profundity of the original. That depth prevents another error as easy as the first and perhaps more dangerous. It is comparatively easy to train the mind to remember that the nature of God is not primarily spatial; it is not quite so easy to remember that it is not primarily paternal—that is, that he does not exist primarily for us. No doubt we are, and can only be, concerned with the way in which he exists for us. The metaphorical use of the word way, in its ordinary sense, contains the other. 'I am the way' is no less 'I am the way in which God exists in relation to men' than 'I am the way by which men exist in relation to God'. But there is a distinction between the idea that God exists primarily for us, and the idea that God exists primarily for himself. The original opening of the Lord's Prayer implies that the paternity of the first two words exists only in the beatitude of the sixth—'Our Father which art in heaven'. The distinction is not merely pedantic; it encourages in adoration a style of intelligence and humility. It restores again the lucid contemplation which is epigrammatized in such a phrase as (Izaak Walton tells us) was loved and used by John Donne 'in a kind of sacred extasie—*Blessed be God that he is God only and divinely like himself*'.

This heaven which is beatitude is further defined by the

second clause in which the word occurs in the Lord's Prayer: 'Thy will be done on earth as it is in heaven.' It is habitually assumed that the second part of the clause refers to the beings—angels or other—who possess heaven as a place or are possessed by it as a state. The will that is to be fulfilled on earth is regarded as relating to other events and possibilities than those which are covered in heaven by the will already fulfilled. But in fact there is another possible meaning. The fulfilment of the will in heaven may grammatically relate to us as well as to angels. The events for which we sincerely implore that fulfilment upon earth are already perfectly concluded by it in heaven. Their conclusions have to be known by us on earth, but they already exist as events in heaven. Heaven, that is to say, possesses timelessness; it has the quality of eternity, of (in the definition which Boethius passed on to Aquinas) 'the perfect and simultaneous possession of everlasting life'. In that simultaneity the passion of the prayer is already granted; all that is left for us to do is to discover in the process of time the conclusion that we have implored in time. 'Let us', the clause demands, in this understanding, 'know thy will being done upon earth as, in this very event, it is already perfectly done and perfectly known in heaven—in the beatitude which is of thee.' This is the consummation of act in belief—in 'faith'.

Heaven then is beatitude and the eternal fulfilment of the Will, the contemporaneousness of perfection. As a state (or a place) in possible relation with us it was created by the Will: 'Maker of heaven and earth.' But the Creeds which declare this declare also something of the relation. They declare a process, though (it is true) in spatial metaphors: 'who for us men and for our salvation came down from heaven. . . . He ascended into heaven.' There emerges and returns from that state of eternal beatitude something or someone charged with a particular intention towards men. It is obvious that this must be related to the doing of the Will, because (on the general definition) there is nothing else that can emerge from and return to that state. Of the possibility of that emergence and return, this is not the immediate place to speak. It is obvious that, however we define

heaven—spiritually or spatially—the word earth does in fact
mean both. Earth is to us inevitably a place, but it is, also
inevitably, the only state which we know, our spiritual state
within that place. The identification of the two as earth has no
doubt assisted us to see both spatial and spiritual meanings in the
word heaven. But heaven is distinguished from earth, and earth
at the moment may be taken to mean that place and state which
have not the eternity of heaven. If it has a perfection, it is a
temporal perfection, a perfection known in sequence. The Will
emerges from the heaven of its beatitude (and the beatitude of
all creatures existing in their mode of perfect relation to it) and
returns thither. Of that Will, so emerging and returning, it is
said: 'The kingdom of heaven is at hand'; it is called 'the
kingdom of heaven' in that activity.

Religion is the definition of that relationship. The records of
it, as it has been understood by Christendom, are contained
formally in two sets of documents: (i) the Canonical Scriptures,
that is, the Bible; (ii) the Rituals of the Church. Neither is complete alone, nor can be understood alone. So far as they can be
separated, it might be said that the Bible, up to and including
the Acts of the Apostles, is concerned rather with *what happened*, the Rituals with *what is happening*. The Epistles belong
to both. It is true that all that did happen is a presentation of
what is happening; all the historical events, especially of this
category, are a pageant of the events of the human soul. But it is
true also that Christendom has always held that the two are
indissolubly connected; that the events in the human soul could
not exist unless the historical events had existed. If, *per impossible*, it could be divinely certain that the historical events upon
which Christendom reposes had not yet happened, all that could
be said would be that they had not *yet* happened. If time and
place are wrong, they are at least all that can be wrong. If, by a
wild fantasy, the foundations of Christendom are not yet dug,
then we have only the architect's plan. But those foundations
can never be dug on any other plan. The passion—often the too-
angry passion—with which the orthodox have defended a
doctrine such as the Virgin Birth has (apart from mystical inter-

12

pretation and vicious obstinacy) this consummation of the historical sense as its chief cause. The union of history and the individual is, like that of so many other opposites, in the coming of the kingdom of heaven, historic and contemporary at once. It was historic in order that it might always be contemporary; it is contemporary because it was certainly historic.

It is the Bible which describes and defines for us the coming of the kingdom, and by the Bible is meant for this book the English version, the Authorized supplemented by the Revised. It is, whether fortunately or unfortunately, that source from which the English imagination has for centuries received the communication of Christendom, and from which the Christian imagination in England still, commonly and habitually, derives. No doubt this derivation is, to a large extent, governed by the doctrines of the Catholic Church. But it is a fact that most English minds still interested in Christendom regard the Bible and the Church rather as allied and intermingled organisms than the Church as the single organism producing the Bible as a part of its inspired activity. That is why it will be convenient here to follow the complex imagination contained in the phrase 'came down from heaven' as it is derived from the Bible. It is the habit nowadays to talk of the Bible as great literature; the Bible-worship of our forefathers has been succeeded by a more misguided and more offensive solemnity of conditioned respect, as accidentally uncritical as deliberately irreligious. Uncritical, because too often that literary respect is oddly conditioned by an ignoring of the book's main theme.

It has certainly many minor themes. Like all the rest of English literature, it consists of a multitude of arrangements of English words expressing, with very great poignancy, various states of being. They are expressed in many different conventions—in narrative, in dialogue, in lyric; in histories, in letters, in schedules and codes of law; in fantasies of apocalypse and myths of creation. Many are familiar enough—the devotion of Ruth, the impatience of Job, the distress of David, the passion of the Shulamite; others are less familiar. The whole of the Bible is a nexus of states of being; a pattern developed in a

13

proper sequence from its bare opening through all its enlarging theme. It even involves states of being more than individual; it concerns itself with corporations and companies. Setting aside supernatural beings, the central figure of the Old Testament is Israel; the central figure of the New is the Church. Those companies dominate their members, except when some peculiarly poignant state of individual being emerges, and by sheer power momentarily dominates the mass. Even then the moment of individuality illuminates and returns to the mass; it is never forgotten that the Israelites are members of the nation as the believers are of the Church, and it is the greater organism which is the full subject, at whatever time. Through those greater organisms, as through the many lesser, there arises a sense of corporate mankind. Individuals and companies, and mankind itself, are all finally set in relation to that non-human cause and centre which is called God.

For the central theme is made up of the lesser themes and of something more, and as in all great literature the lesser themes are there to help compose the greater. The whole Canon signifies a particular thing—the original nature of man, the entrance of contradiction into his nature, and the manner of his restoration. If this theme is ignored the Bible as a whole cannot be understood as literature. By a deprivation of the central idea, and of the personification of that idea, the Bible does not cease to be metaphysics and become literature; it ceases to be anything at all but little bits of literature rather oddly collated. But without that deprivation it is literature related to the greatest of human themes—the nature of man and his destiny. Its doctrine may be wrong, but without its doctrine it is, as a book, nothing. It deals no longer with mankind, as is pretended, only with a number of men. To alter it so may be a moral virtue, but it certainly is not good literary criticism.

Yet it is precisely good literary criticism which is needed, for those of us who are neither theologians, higher critics, nor fundamentalists; that is, for most of us. We are concerned, if we are concerned at all, to know what the book is at, as much as to know what *King Lear* or the *Prelude* is at, and that can only be done by the methods of literary criticism, by the contemplation of the states of being the book describes, by the relation of phrase to phrase and the illumination of phrase by phrase, by the discovery (without ingenuity) of complexity within complexity and simplicity within simplicity. There is simply no other way to go about it, because it consists of words. Bible-reading and meditation must be based on words; they are meant to extract the utmost possible meaning out of words. Certainly there are some books whose words, once we have studied them, seem to demand from us a moral, even a metaphysical, assent or dissent. Literary criticism, that is, may lead to or even be transmuted into something more intense even than itself. Such books are the *Pilgrim's Progress* and the *Divine Comedy* and the *De Natura Rerum* and the Bible. They become something more in the same way that the crowd around Messias were suddenly exhibited in an office and authority unexpected when he looked on them and cried out 'Behold my mother and my brethren.' But that declaration of their maternity did not alter their original humanity, and so with the words of these books.

There is, in especial, one law of literary criticism which is of use—the law of emptying the words. Everyone who has studied great verse knows how necessary is the effort to clear the mind of our own second-hand attribution of meanings to words in order that the poet may fill them with *his* meanings. No less care is needed in reading the Bible. Some form, of course, each word must retain, some shape and general direction. But its general colour is, naturally, only learnt from its use throughout. This has to be discovered. As a fact words such as 'faith', 'pardon', or 'glory' are taken with meanings borrowed from the common-place of everyday; comparatively few readers set to work to find out what the Bible means by them. The word 'love' has suffered even more heavily. The famous saying 'God is love', it is generally assumed, means that God is like our immediate emotional indulgence, and not that our meaning of love ought to have something of the 'otherness' and terror of God.

Acknowledging therefore the general meaning of a few words as they occur, and even charging (if desirable) the word heaven

15

when it occurs with all requisite power, it may be permissible to examine briefly a few other words and events contained in the Bible, in relation to the clause 'who . . . came down from heaven'. At its beginning the Bible knows very little of the meaning of words. All great art creates, as it were, its own stillness about it, but by the nature of its subject the Bible does more. It opens with a single rift of light striking along the darkness which existed before words were: 'In the beginning God created the heavens and the earth.'

CHAPTER II

The Myth of the Alteration in Knowledge

The word 'God' in the opening sentences of Genesis is practically characterless. It means only That which creates, and what it creates is good in its own eyes. The diagram of the six days develops with a geometrical precision, measured by the ambiguous word 'Day'. To give that word the meaning merely of the passage of a myriad years is impossible, so much is it defined by its recurrent evenings and mornings; it is nearer our twenty-four hour day than anything else. Yet time is pressed into it; it has a double relationship of duration, divine and human; and it repeats itself as a refrain of mathematical incantation—the first calculation and the first ritual. Along that rift of light, according to the double pulsing sound —'the evening and the morning were the Day'; 'God saw that it was good'—the geometry of creation enlarges. The universe exists, and earth, and the seas, and all creatures. But there is no further explanation of the God.

The heavens are here, no doubt, spatial skies in relation to spatial earth, and the earth is the place of limited perfection in time. Man exists upon earth, and with his appearance the imagination finds that it has abandoned its standpoint at the beginning of that primal ray, and has removed itself to earth. It is the opening of the great myth of man's origins. Earth exists and is good; the man and woman—the Adam—exist and are good; and their whole state is good.[1] It is not less good because

[1] There is a reading which takes the 'going up of the mist' to be a clouding of creation, after which the separation of the Adam into two creatures took place. But it is not possible in this book to ascend to such speculations. I follow everywhere the most commonplace interpretation.

there exists a prohibition. But the myth makes use of the prohibition to proceed to its account of the Fall.

There are, roughly, two bases for the idea of the Fall. One is
the general Judaeo-Christian tradition; the other is the facts of
present human existence. Both bases will be rejected by those
who have already rejected their fundamental hypotheses. The
first depends upon the whole doctrine of the Christian Church,
and is a corollary of that doctrine. The second depends upon the
hypotheses of an omnipotent and benevolent God and of man's
free will. 'Either there is no Creator (in that sense) *or* the living
society of men is in a true sense discarded from his presence',
said Newman. Something must have gone wrong somewhere.
If (on the hypothesis) it cannot have gone wrong with God, it
must have gone wrong with us. If heaven is a name for a state of
real perfection, we ourselves have most remarkably 'come down
from heaven'.

This necessity of thought has been generally accepted by the
Christian Church, though the Church has never defined the
nature of that aboriginal catastrophe the tale of which it accepts.
It has traditionally rather accepted the view that this catastrophe
was the second of its kind, the first having occurred in the
'heavens' themselves, and among those creatures whom we call
angels. Our own awareness of this explanation is generally
referred to the genius of Milton, who certainly shaped it for us
in great poetry and made use of it to express his own tender
knowledge of the infinite capacity of man's spirit for foolish
defiance of the God. But long before Milton the strange tale
recedes, and long before Milton the prayers of Christendom
implore aid against the malignity of fallen spirits. The popularity of the legend has perhaps been assisted by the excuse it
has seemed to offer for mankind, by the pseudo-answer it has
appeared to offer to the difficulty of the philosophical imagination concerning a revolt in the good against the good, and by
its provision of a figure or figures against whom men can, on
the highest principles, launch their capacities of indignant hate
and romantic fear. The devil, even if he is a fact, has been an
indulgence; he has, on occasion, been encouraged to reintroduce

into Christian emotions the dualism which the Christian intellect has denied, and we have relieved our own sense of moral submission by contemplating, even disapprovingly, something which was neither moral nor submissive. An 'inferiority complex', in the slang of our day, is not the same thing as humility; the devil has often been the figure of the first, a reverse from the second, and the frontier between the two. While he exists there is always something to which we can be superior.

Of all this, however, the book of Genesis knows nothing (unless, indeed, in the sentence about the mist). The myth of the Fall there is formally limited to the Adam, and to the creature 'of the field', an immense subtlety twining into speech. There is not much difference apparently between the Adam and the beasts, except that he (or they) control them. There is nothing about intellectual power; in fact, so far as their activities in Genesis are concerned, the intelligence of the Adam is limited to preserving their lives by obtaining food, by a capacity for agriculture, and by a clear moral sense, though behind these things lies the final incantation of the creation: 'Let us make man in Our image, after Our likeness', and the decision upon that, as upon the earliest rift of light: 'behold, it was very good'.

The nature of the Fall—both while possible and when actual —is clearly defined. The 'fruit of the tree' is to bring an increase of knowledge. That increase, however, is, and is desired as being, of a particular kind. It is not merely to know more, but to know in another method. It is primarily the advance (if it can be so called) from knowing good to knowing good and evil; it is (secondarily) the knowing 'as gods': A certain knowledge was, by its nature, confined to divine beings. Its communication to man would be, by its nature, disastrous to man. The Adam had been created and were existing in a state of knowledge of good and nothing but good. They knew that there was some kind of alternative, and they knew that the rejection of the alternative was part of their relation to the Omnipotence that created them. That relation was part of the good they enjoyed. But they knew also that the knowledge in the Omnipotence was greater than their own; they understood that in some way it knew 'evil'.

He came down from Heaven

It was, in future ages, declared by Aquinas that it was of the nature of God to know all possibilities, and to determine which possibility should become fact. 'God would not know good things perfectly, unless he also knew evil things . . . for, since evil is not of itself knowable, forasmuch as "evil is the privation of good", as Augustine says (*Confess.* iii, 7), therefore evil can neither be defined nor known except by good.' Things which are not and never will be he knows 'not by vision', as he does all things that are, or will be, 'but by simple intelligence'. It is therefore part of that knowledge that he should understand good in its deprivation, the identity of heaven in its opposite identity of hell, but without 'approbation', without calling it into being at all.

It was not so possible for man, and the myth is the tale of that impossibility. However solemn and intellectual the exposition of the act sounds, the act itself is simple enough. It is easy for us now, after the terrible and prolonged habit of mankind; it was not, perhaps, very difficult then—as easy as picking a fruit from a tree. It was merely to wish to know an antagonism in the good, to find out what the good would be like if a contradiction were introduced into it. Man desired to know schism in the universe. It was a knowledge reserved to God; man had been warned that he could not bear it—'in the day that thou eatest thereof thou shalt surely die'. A serpentine subtlety over-whelmed that statement with a grander promise—'Ye shall be as gods, knowing good and evil'. Unfortunately to be as gods meant, for the Adam, to die, for to know evil, for them, was to know it not by pure intelligence but by experience. It was, precisely, to experience the opposite of good, that is the depriva-tion of the good, the slow destruction of the good, and of them-selves with the good.

The Adam were permitted to achieve this knowledge if they wished; they did so wish. Some possibility of opposite action there must be if there is to be any relation between different wills. Free will is a thing incomprehensible to the logical mind, and perhaps not very often possible to the human spirit. The glasses of water which we are so often assured that we can or can

20

not drink do not really refract light on the problem. '*Nihil sumus nisi voluntates*', said Augustine, but the thing we fundamentally are is not easily known. Will is rather a thing we may choose to become than a thing we already possess—except so far as we can a little choose to choose, a little will to will. The Adam, with more will, exercised will in the myth. They knew good; they wished to know good and evil. Since there was not—since there never has been and never will be—anything else than the good to know, they knew good as antagonism. All difference consists in the mode of knowledge. They had what they wanted. That they did not like it when they got it does not alter the fact that they certainly got it.

The change in knowledge is indicated by one detail. The tale presents the Adam as naked, and in a state of enjoyment of being naked. It was part of their good; they had delight in their physical natures. There is no suggestion that they had not a delight in their sexual natures and relationship. They had about them a free candour, and that candour of joy was a part of their good. They were not ashamed. They then insisted on knowing good as evil; and they did. They knew that candour as undesirable; they experienced shame. The Omnipotence might intelligently know what the deprivation of that candour would be like, and yet not approve it into existence. The divine prerogative could not enter other beings after that manner; they had to know after their own nature. The thing they had involved confused them, because its nature was confusion. Sex had been good; it became evil. They made themselves aprons. It was exactly what they had determined. Since then it has often been thought that we might recover the single and simple knowledge of good in that respect by tearing up the aprons. It has never, so far, been found that the return is quite so easy. To revoke the knowledge of unlovely shame can only be done by discovering a loveliness of shame (not necessarily that shame, but something more profound) in the good. The Lord, it may be remarked, did not make aprons for the Adam; he made them coats. He was not so sex-conscious as some of the commentators, pious and other.

He came down from Heaven

Another detail is in the interrogation in the garden. It is the conclusion of the first great episode in the myth of origin. The decision has, inevitably, changed the relationship of the Adam to the Omnipotence. It is in the garden and they are afraid. As they have a shameful modesty towards each other, so they have an evil humility towards the Creator. They do not think it tolerable that they should be seen as they are. Unfortunately the interrogation merely exhibits them as they are; a severe actuality is before them, and they dislike it. They know evil; that is, they know the good of fact as repugnant to them. They are forced into it. The well-meaning comment which blames Adam for telling tales about the woman overlooks the fact that he had no choice. In schools and in divorce-courts we used to be taught to lie on a woman's behalf; the fashion of morals may now have changed. But Adam is not in that kind of divorce-court. He has been dragged out from among the concealing trees of the garden, he is riddled now with a new mode of knowledge, but the old knowledge is forced to speak. The full result of their determination is exhibited. 'Ye shall be as gods, knowing good and evil.' So you shall. Sorrow and conception; the evil of the ground; the sorrow of life; the hardship of toil; all things in antagonism and schism; love a distress and labour a grief; all the good known in the deprivation of the good, in the deprivation of joy. Only the death which the serpent had derided returns to them as mercy; they are not, at least, to live for ever; the awful possibility of Eden is removed. They are to be allowed to die.

The contradiction in the nature of man is thus completely established. He knows good, and he knows good as evil. These two capacities will always be present in him; his love will always be twisted with anti-love, with anger, with spite, with jealousy, with alien desires. Lucidity and confusion are alike natural, and there is no corner into which antagonism to pure joy has not broken. It is in the episode of Cain and Abel that this alteration of knowledge is most exhibited. It is shown also in a new development. The original tale had dealt almost wholly with the relation of the Adam to the Omnipotence; their rela-

22

tion between themselves had not been much considered. But the next generation sees a schism in mankind itself. The objection mostly raised to that episode of the myth is to the sacrifice of the 'firstlings of the flock'. It is a natural objection, and it certainly has to be left unanswered or answered only by the comment that from beginning to end the Bible is negligent of a great deal of our humane instincts. Man having got himself into a state when he was capable of willingly shedding blood, the shedding of blood could no longer be neglected. That pouring out of the blood 'which is life' was bound to become a central thing, for it was the one final and utterly irrevocable thing. It is that which Adam offers to the Lord, and which the Lord accepts. Cain himself seems to have had no humanitarian objections, or if he had they did not extend to his relations. But the main point is the first breach in humanity, the first outrage against *pietas*, and (more importantly) the first imagined proclamation of *pietas* from the heavens—from the skies or from eternal perfection. 'Am I my brother's keeper?' 'The voice of thy brother's blood crieth unto me from the ground. And now art thou cursed from the earth.' Human relationship has become to a man a source of anger and hate, and the hatred in its turn brings more desolation. It is the opening of the second theme of the Bible—the theme of *pietas* and the community. The curse of the primeval choice is now fully at work, and the great myth passes on to the first hint of the resolution of the lasting crisis of that curse.

The first book, as it were, of the myth is taken up by the entrance of contradiction into the spirit of man. The second is the period of the covenants. So far there has been no development of the character of the God; not, anyhow, in so many words. It is possible to make deductions, such as to observe Messianic prophecies from the talk of the head and the heel in the garden of Eden, and to discern a careful Providence in the making of coats of skins. But these are rather the drawing of what Wordsworth called 'the sustaining thought' from the progress of the tale, and Wordsworth, like any other great writer (even the author, no doubt, of the book of Genesis), distinguished carefully between tales and sustaining thoughts drawn from tales. The second are much more patient of our own interpretations than the first, and there has so far been little interpretation of God in Genesis itself; no more, perhaps, than the implication that he is concerned at the breach of human relations in the murder of Abel. But now—by how little, yet by how much!—there is an alteration. The single rift of pure light in which all that has happened has so far been seen—the identities of heaven and earth, and man setting antagonism in his mind towards them, Adam and Eve passing over the earth, and Cain flying into the wilderness—this lies upon the Flood and changes. The pure light of mere distinction between God and man changes; it takes on colour and becomes prismatic with the rainbow. The very style of the Bible itself changes; the austere opening pulsates with multiplied relationships. Man becomes men.

The first covenant is that with Noah. It begins by repeating the single gift of power with which the Omnipotence had endowed Adam, but it adds to it the threat against Cain, and combines something new of its own. It proclaims a law: 'At the hand of every man's brother will I require the life of man.' It is a declaration of an exchange of responsibility rather than of joy, but the web of substitution is to that extent created, however distant from the high end and utter conclusion of entire interchange. Into the chaotic experience of good as evil the first pattern of order is introduced; every man is to answer for the life of his brother. As the Omnipotence so limits man, it limits itself, and for the first time characterizes itself by a limitation— 'the everlasting convenant between God and every living creature of all flesh that is upon the earth'. It consents to agreement, to limitation, to patience, patience which is here the first faint hint of a thing yet unknown to the myth, the first preluding check on that activity of power which is presently to become a new mode of power—grace.

The second covenant is that made with Abraham, and afterwards renewed with Isaac and Jacob. It comes after the destruction of Babel; that symbolic legend of the effort man makes to approach heaven objectively only, as by the vain effort of the removal of aprons. It is a recurrent effort, since it is a recurrent temptation: if this or that could be done, surely the great tower would arise, and we should walk in heaven among gods—as when the orthodox of any creed think that all will be well when their creed is universal. Yet the recurrent opposite is no more true, for unless something is done, nothing happens. Unless devotion is given to a thing which must prove false in the end, the thing that is true in the end cannot enter. But the distinction between necessary belief and unnecessary credulity is as necessary as belief; it is the heightening and purifying of belief. There is nothing that matters of which it is not sometimes desirable to feel: 'this does not matter'. 'This also is Thou; neither is this Thou.' But it may be admitted also that this is part of the technique of belief in our present state; not even Isaiah or Aquinas have pursued to its revelation the mystery of self-scepticism in the divine. The nearest, perhaps, we can get to that is in the incredulous joy of great romantic moments—in love or poetry or what else: 'this cannot possibly be, and it is'. Usually the way must be made ready for heaven, and then it will come by some other; the sacrifice must be made ready, and the fire will strike on another altar. So much Cain saw, and could not guess that the very purpose of his offering was to make his brother's acceptable.

Babel had fallen, and the nations and peoples of the earth were established, in variation of speech and habit like the rainbow of the covenant above them. Out of that covenant a new order issues, and the first great formula of salvation. It is the promise and first establishment of Israel, but of Israel in a formula which applies both to it and to the future company of the New Testament, the Church. 'I will bless thee . . . thou shalt be a blessing . . . in thee shall all families of the earth be blessed' (Gen. xii, 1–3). Israel is to be exclusive and inclusive at once, like all modes of redemption, particular and universal. Their inclusive-exclusive statement is retained in the repetitions of the covenants, and it is permitted to become indeed a covenant. The covenant with Noah had been rather a one-sided promise than a covenant, but now a sign is established. Besides the exchange of responsibility, the *pietas* between man and man, there is to be a particular mode of adoration, ritual and deliberately ritual. It is the exclusive sign which is to be inclusive in its effects. The uncircumcized child is to be cut off from the people, yet all the earth is again to know beatitude. The mysterious promise of blessing is to be established in that intimate body of man which had, in the old myth, swallowed the fatal fruit: 'my covenant shall be in your flesh'. The precise declaration is renewed to the generations; the single is to be a blessing to all.

There are two points here which may be remarked in the mere manner of the myth. The first relates to what are usually called the anthropomorphic appearances of the God. There is no doubt that they happen, but the point is that they are precisely appearances. They are rare, and they are condescensions. They succeed in their effectiveness because they are unusual condescensions. The God of Genesis is not a kind of supernatural man; he is something quite different which occasionally deigns to appear like a supernatural man. Something unlike man behaves like man. It exists; it breaks off. 'And the Lord went his way . . . and Abraham returned unto his place.'

The second point refers to a question of style. The climax of those anthropomorphic appearances is in that most admirably composed passage of words with Abraham concerning Sodom. Up to then the few conversations between man and the Omnipotence have been extremely one-sided. But now there appears something new: the conversation becomes a dialogue. The remoteness and rigour of the Lord take on a tenderness— almost (but for the terror of the subject) a laughter—and there exists not only a promise but a reply. The promise, that is, becomes a fuller and richer thing; it is the whole meaning of prayer. Prayer, like everything else, was meant for a means of joy; but, in our knowledge of the good as evil, we have to recover it so, and it is not an easy thing. Prayer is thought of as a means to an end, but the end itself is sometimes only the means to the means, as with all love. The fantastic intercession of Abraham dances and retreats and salaams and dances again; and the thunder that threatens on the left the Cities of the Plain

The Myth of the Alteration in Knowledge

murmurs gently on the right above the tents. 'And the Lord went his way.'

The myth draws to a conclusion with what may, or may not, be a beginning of history, and yet at that beginning renews its full splendour of style. The last great outbreak of legend is laid among recognizable peoples and familiar titles. Kings and wizards, priests and prophets, caravans and armies, rich men and slaves, are habitual upon earth; something infinitely various is to be offered to the Lord. Such individual moments as the passion of Jacob for Rachel or of Rebekah for Jacob appear; though the numinous appearances linger, as in the figure that strives with Jacob. The inclusive-exclusive thing is followed in its wanderings among the other existences, who do not know it and are to be blessed through it. But now something else has developed on the earth, the impiety of which Cain was the first incarnation. The development of man into peoples has developed also the dark fact of contradiction, and the law of exchange of responsibility is now outraged nationally as well as individually. The rejection of Joseph by his brethren expands into the slavery of the Israelites among the Egyptians. Impiety has reached through the whole social order, and the power of tyranny is established as an accepted thing in the world. It is exceptionally, in this instance, related to the 'chosen people', the means of returning beatitude, and it is in relation to the same people that, in the midst of so much evil still preferred, the God characterizes himself still further. He utters the first grand· metaphysical phrase: the 'I am that I am'. Coleridge, as a poet as well as a philosopher, declared that it should be: 'I am in that I am'. But the alteration is sufficiently given in the message to Pharaoh: 'the I am hath sent me unto you'. The colours of the rainbows are assumed again into a clear light, and the God is no longer only creative but self-existent. It is this utter self-existence the sound of which is prolonged now through the whole book; 'I am the Lord' rings everywhere like the refrain of the heavens.

The first work of that declared self-existence is to free the inclusive-exclusive thing upon earth; indeed, it proclaims itself in the course of that freeing. There emerges at that moment a thing of which Christendom has never lost the vision or the tradition—revolution. The tale of it here may be incredible; it may even be disbelieved. The launching of the plagues on the land of Egypt, the hardening of the heart of Pharaoh into the thing that Pharaoh himself has wished, the locusts and the frogs and the Nile as blood—all these may be the romantic decorations of the legend. In effect the answer of Pharaoh is common enough: 'We will chance all that rather than let the people go' —till the dead lie in the streets of the cities. The vision of those streets has remained. In the night of death, when all the hopes and heirs of Egypt lie motionless, the victims of impiety are redeemed. The dispossessed and the rejected are in movement through the whole land. Renounce the myth and the vision remains. There is flung out for us the image of the great host, bribed and adorned with the jewels of their taskmasters, marching out under the prophet and the priest and the woman; marching under the fire and the cloud of the terrible covenanted God. 'I am that I am'; 'I am the Lord'. The heavens go before the host, the habitation of the proceeding Power, and of the single voice in and beyond creation that is able to proclaim its own identity, the voice of the original good. They pour on; the waters stand up to let them pass, and nature is hurled back for the departure of the slaves. 'Why callest thou upon me? speak unto the children of Israel that they go forward.' It is the law of exchange that advances, of the keeping of one life by another, of the oath that cannot be controlled by man; it is the knowledge of good as good breaking out of the knowledge of good as evil. 'The Egyptians shall know that I am the Lord when I have gotten me honour upon Pharaoh, upon his chariots, and upon his horsemen.' In a symbol of universal application, the angel of the Lord and the cloud of heaven stand between the two hosts, and between the two methods of knowledge, and the sea roars down. In the morning the chariots and bodies of the dead are tossed on the shore, and the timbrels of the singing women mock at the wreckage of the possessors and the rich, while the shout of the free people adores the Divine salvation.

CHAPTER III

The Mystery of Pardon and the Paradox of Vanity

It is perhaps worth pausing before considering certain aspects of the Prophets, upon another book of the Old Testament. Between the group of books which is mainly mythical and historic and the group which is mainly lyric and prophetic lies, at the centre of the Old Testament, the book of Job. The book of Job, as every one knows owing to the popularity of the Bible as literature, is a very remarkable work. There seems to be a general indefinite opinion that it only got into the Bible by accident, and that its author would be astonished and perhaps ashamed if he could know his companions. Certainly it is thought that the author of most of the book would be ashamed of the author of the last chapter, who provided Job with a happy ending, much as Shakespeare provided reckless marriages—the official equivalent of a happy ending—in so many of his last acts.

At the risk of contumely, however, it remains possible to consider Job as an English book. The adept critics may object, but hardly anyone else dare, for fear a little further criticism should undercut their own position. For the author of the last chapter added one important thing to the Bible, a thing implicit in the rest of Job and indeed in much else of the Bible, but hardly so adequately defined anywhere else—except, indeed, by the Virgin Mary. His work has saved Christendom from being misled by Saint Paul's rash refusal to allow the thing formed to ask questions of him that formed it, the pot of the potter: one of those metaphors which miss the bull while thudding the target, like the often-repeated comparison between the Church and a club. No club (however Right or however Left or however Central—not even the Sodality of Saint Thomas Didymus, Apostle and Sceptic) claims to be possessed of the only certain means of salvation. No pot—so far—has asked questions of the potter in a voice the potter can understand; when it does, it will be time enough to compare pots to men. The criticism is not aimed at Saint Paul who dropped the phrase in the midst of a great spiritual wrestle, not as a moral instruction. But it has been used too often by the pious to encourage them to say, in love or in laziness, 'Our little minds were never meant . . .' Fortunately there is the book of Job to make it clear that our little minds were meant. A great curiosity ought to exist concerning divine things. Man was intended to argue with God.

It is an odd comment on our reading of original texts (and not only the text of the Bible) to remember that one of the commonest phrases in the language attributes patience to Job. Any reader who, with that in his mind, turns to the words which Job actually utters will find that, after a single rebuke to his wife for advising him to curse God, he plunges into a series of demands on and accusations of God which may be and indeed are epigrams of high intelligence, but are not noticeably patient. It is indeed his impatience which his friends find shameful in him. He who has been not only a prince of this world, but also in his righteousness almost a prince of heaven, who has not only served God himself but has interceded for others, whose tragedy has conformed (though they could not know it) almost to Aristotle's rules, ruins both Greek form and Jewish piety by hurling accusations against the Immortal. He does not merely blame God on his own behalf; he denounces God's way with mankind.

An analysis of the whole book has been supplied often enough, and in default of any convenient analysis there is even the book itself to be read. The first point here is the bitterness of the accusation: 'He will laugh at the trial of the innocent'; 'is it good unto thee that thou shouldest oppress?'; 'he removeth away the speech of the trusty, and taketh away the understanding of the aged'. The second is the demand for some kind of equality:

The Mystery of Pardon and the Paradox of Vanity

'Let him take away his rod from me, and let not his fear terrify me, then would I speak and not fear him'; 'O that I knew where I might find him! that I might come even to his seat! I would order my cause before him, and fill my mouth with argument'; 'behold, my desire is, that the Almighty would answer me'. If God will make himself man's equal—so, if not, there is no sense in talking. Let him submit himself to question, but does he? no; 'he taketh away the understanding of the aged'.

The stark rage of Job produces, in the pause that follows the whole argument, an answering rage in the universe; there breaks out of the air about the disputants a storm of taunts. The air itself is twisted and swept into a whirlwind, as if something within it drove outwards; an effect rare but magnificent in literature, as when Dante in the Earthly Paradise sees lights that seem to emerge from within the air rather than to advance through it. The veil of creation dissolves, and the images worked on it become living and doubly mighty in the voice that summons them. The Lord declines altogether to withdraw his hand or to modify his nature. He speaks irrationally; he offers no kind of intelligent explanation. But the main point is that he has answered; he has acknowledged Job's claim even if only to rail at it. His mockeries are themselves a reply. It is true he says nothing new—nothing that Job has not already said. 'Canst thou bind the sweet influences of Pleiades, or loose the bands of Orion? canst thou bring forth Mazzaroth in his season? or canst thou guide Arcturus with his sons?' Except for Mazzaroth, the Lord is only plagiarizing here from Job, who had already said of him: 'which maketh Arcturus, Orion, and Pleiades, and the chambers of the south'. The whole force of the conclusion is in the fact that it is a reply.

But the reply is not confined to Job. The three friends who have been defending orthodoxy and assuring Job of his sinfulness have their reward. 'Ye have not spoken of me the thing that is right as my servant Job hath.' Job is to sacrifice and intercede for them, 'lest I deal with you after your folly'. The pretence that we must not ask God what he thinks he is doing (and is therefore doing) is swept away. The Lord demands that his

31

people shall demand an explanation from him. Whether they understand it or like it when they get it is another matter, but demand it they must and shall. Humility has never consisted in not asking questions; it does not make men less themselves or less intelligent, but more intelligent and more themselves. 'And the Lord turned the captivity of Job, when he prayed for his friends; also the Lord gave Job twice as much as he had before.' It is the intercession, then, which marks the moment of return; the salvation of Job from his distress is at the time of interchange. But it was Job's philosophical impatience of angry curiosity that brought him to such a moment. Such a philosophical curiosity is carried on into the New Testament. It accompanies the Annunciation. The Blessed Virgin answered the angelic proclamation with a question: 'How shall these things be?' And of the inhabitants of heaven themselves it is said that 'these things the angels desire to look into'.

The whirlwind of Job is related to another exposition of the heavens—the darkness and fire of Sinai. Sinai in the Bible is the conclusion of the legends and the beginning of the laws. Moses went up into the Mount as myth; he descended as moral teacher. He was a leader in both periods, but there was a difference—as there is a difference in the God to whom he went and the people to whom he returned. The vision of the people as a host marching does not preclude the vision of the people as a mere mob, and it is the mob who become manifest during the dwelling of Moses in the Mount. It is the aggregate of uncertain multitudes and uncertain men; it sways to and fro. This change of value repeats itself continually in the history of the children of Israel.[1] It is that change and change back which are responsible for the recurrent phrase 'the Lord repented him', which is nonsense and truth at once. It is, as a phrase, the continuation of the dialogue with Abraham, the promise as a reply; the prelude of something yet deeper and still to be; the hint of the self-limitation of the

[1] Any book which has occasion to refer often to the Israelites must feel the need of some kind of apology to the Jews. No Englishman could be expected to enjoy such a continual easy discussion of his forefathers by minds of a different culture, and no apology can quite excuse it. Even its inevitability hardly does so.

first covenant carried on to the subordination of the far east. The Will of the Omnipotence is to be turned aside and to submit itself. 'The Lord repented him.'

But while the people become the mob, the idea of the people is illuminated in the Mount. On the arrival at Sinai the salvation of Israel is defined: 'Ye shall be unto me a kingdom of priests and an holy nation.' It is one of the great dreams—a people, a nation, a city, a group, any community great or small—a world of intermediaries, communicating to each other the holy and awful Rites, and yet those Rites (in that state of being) no stranger than common things; the ordinary and extraordinary made extraordinary and ordinary by joy. The means of the coming of this kingdom of priests is in the law, and the law is a movement towards the reconciliation of the divided knowledge, the expulsion of the contradiction from man's nature, the discovery once more of the good as pure good. The I AM (and indeed, all life) is experienced in an evil manner, but the I AM has sworn that he and it shall be known as good, and only good, to whoever chooses. The first step is the re-creation of an order in confusion, so that a more than social distinction shall be made. It is important to maintain the *pietas* towards man, but no less the acknowledgement and adoration of the complex thing of heaven.

It is this law and the covenant of which it is a part which the prophets, later, guard. They are the keepers of the contract; they preserve the relations of the I AM with the people. They preserve also the vision of the glory of the I AM. The word glory, to English ears, usually means no more than a kind of mazy bright blur. But the maze should be, though it generally is not, exact, and the brightness should be that of a geometrical pattern. It is this which becomes a kind of key problem—what is the web of the glory of heaven as a state? It may be said, roughly, that certain patterns in the web are already discernible: the recognition of the good, everywhere and always, as good, the reflection of power, the exercise of intellect, the importance of interchange, and a deliberate relation to the Centre. All this is knowledge of good, knowledge of joy, and not only a mental knowledge (though it includes that) but a knowledge through

c   33

every capacity of being. Heaven, one may say, has been (apart
from its spatial meaning) hitherto not much more than the mere
exposition of the I AM; first a rift of light, then a prism of the
colours of divine goodwill, then a light of metaphysical existence. On Sinai the glory is precisely the brightness of that
existence radiated outward. Moses, in a cleft of the rock,
entreats to see the glory, and beholds the God pass by: 'I will
make all my goodness pass before thee . . . thou canst not see my
face: for there shall no man see me and live.' The glory is the
goodness, but even the goodness is not he.

Moses saw it, as it were, simply. Isaiah and Ezekiel see more.
In the sixth chapter of the one, and the first of the other, the
undifferentiated glory of Sinai has become living complexes of
radiancy. The monsters of earth in Job are rivalled in the prophets by monsters of heaven. 'Above it stood the seraphim: each
one had six wings; with twain he covered his face, and with
twain he covered his feet, and with twain he did fly.' 'As for the
likeness of the living creatures, their appearance was like
burning coals of fire, and like the appearance of lamps; it went
up and down among the living creatures; and the fire was
bright, and out of the fire went forth lightning. And the living
creatures ran and returned as the appearance of a flash of lightning. . . . The appearance of the wheels and their work was like
unto the colour of a beryl . . . as it were a wheel in the middle of
a wheel.' 'As for their rings they were so high that they were
dreadful, and their rings were full of eyes.' 'And the likeness of
the firmament upon the heads of the living creatures was as the
colour of the terrible crystal, stretched forth over their wings
above.'

The wheels and the eyes, and the spirit in the wheels, and
their lifting up, have been subject to a good deal of gay humour,
but they are a myth of a vital pattern of organisms. 'God always
geometrizes' said Plato, and the Hebrew prophets thought no
less. There is something more also; round the appearance of a
throne and 'the likeness as the appearance of a man above upon
it' (anthropomorphic creatures!) is the old prism of promise.
The likeness as the appearance of the man is 'as the colour of

amber, as the appearance of fire round about within it' upward from the loins, and downward from 'the appearance' of loins is the appearance of fire 'and it had brightness round about. As the appearance of the bow that is in the cloud in the day of rain, so was the appearance of the brightness round about. This was the appearance of the likeness of the glory of the Lord. And when I saw it I fell upon my face . . . and he said unto me, Son of man, stand upon thy feet, and I will speak with thee.'

The colours of the rainbow had been a witness to the covenant; now they are the accompaniment of that which rides upon the bright mathematics of the company of heaven. Any presentation more reluctant to become anthropomorphic—with its likenesses and its appearances, and its obvious insistence upon them as similes and metaphors—can hardly be imagined. Since, of course, in the end anything that means anything to man has to be in terms of something remotely significant to man, from the wheels of Ezekiel to the vortices of pure thought of Mr. Shaw or the monstrous equations of great science. It is true that in some way or other those earlier mathematics profess a relation to man. On that final grand division there can, it seems, be no compromise; either the Lord is concerned with man in himself or he is not. It is for man to make a fair return by an adoration of the Lord only in himself.

The prophets are sent out from the visible mathematics of the glory to proclaim the moral mathematics of the glory. Morality is either the mathematics of power or it is nothing. Their business is to recover mankind—but first the inclusive-exclusive Israel—to an effort to know only the good. This, in effect, means recognition of the covenant, and obedience to the law. Those who refuse are described in language which precisely carries on the definition of the contradiction involved in the original Fall. 'Woe unto them that call evil good and good evil . . . that are wise in their own eyes and prudent in their own sight.' The Adam had desired to share the knowledge of the God; they had wished to experience good as something else than good, to discover a hostility in the good. So they did. Their descendants, in the situation in which they were involved, had (and have) the same choice. They can prolong the Fall by their will. They can introduce their own prudence and wisdom into the nature of the good. It is something deeper than impiety or immorality, though it involves them. It is the preference of their own wisdom; it is sin.

Sin has many forms, but the work of all is the same—the preference of an immediately satisfying experience of things to the believed pattern of the universe; one may even say, the pattern of the glory. It has, in the prophets as everywhere, two chief modes of existence: impiety against man and impiety against God—the refusal of others and the insistence on the self.

The first of these here is the consent to social injustice, and the personal gain through social injustice. The people which were brought out of slavery in Egypt have deliberately 'called evil good'. The prophets—at most times—use more effective language than the abstract 'social injustice'. What they say is expressed by Amos:

'Hear this, O ye that swallow up the needy, even to make the poor of the land to fail,

'Saying, When will the new moon be gone, that we may sell corn? and the sabbath, that we may set forth wheat, making the ephah small, and the shekel great, and falsifying the balances by deceit?

'That we may buy the poor for silver, and the needy for a pair of shoes; yea, and sell the refuse of the wheat?'

This failure in the communion of justice ruins all the relations between the I AM and the people. Where the oppressed go unrelieved and the princes follow after rewards, the power of the heavens is turned against man, and no kind of adoration will appease it: 'bring no more vain oblations; incense is an abomination . . . it is iniquity, even the solemn meeting. Your new moons and your appointed feasts my soul hateth . . . your hands are full of blood.' Nevertheless the communion of justice is not sufficient in itself; it is to be perfected by adoration. It is man's business not merely to set up a covenant between himself and his brother, to maintain the exchange of responsibility between life and life, but also to keep the covenant between himself and that other mode of being which can only be signified by the fire of amber above the prismatic brightness of heaven. The two kinds of life are to come together. But this other can also be rejected. There is perhaps no better description of this rejection than is given by Ezekiel.

'And he brought me to the door of the court; and when I looked, behold a hole in the wall.

'Then said he unto me, Son of man, dig now in the wall: and when I had digged in the wall, behold a door.

'And he said unto me, Go in, and behold the wicked abominations that they do here.

'So I went in and saw; and behold every form of creeping things, and abominable beasts, and all the idols of the house of Israel, portrayed upon the wall round about.

'And there stood before them seventy men of the ancients of the house of Israel, and in the midst of them stood Jaazaniah the son of Shaphan, with every man his censer in his hand; and a thick cloud of incense went up.

'Then said he unto me, Son of man, hast thou seen what the ancients of the house of Israel do in the dark, every man in the chambers of his imagery? for they say, The Lord seeth us not; the Lord hath forsaken the earth.'

The digging in the wall and the discovery of the secret chamber, the thick incense before the images of creeping things on the wall, the old men swinging thuribles before the shapes of abominable beasts—all this is a significance of choice in terms of adoration. So the rich men waiting for the end of the ritual feasts to trick the markets, to entrap the poor and throw them a few clothes for their lives' labour, to defraud them even then by selling refuse in the place of food—this is a significance of choice in terms of justice. Either way there is the preference of a lie, a desired contradiction, a calling of evil good. It is summed up in Jeremiah: 'a wonderful and horrible thing is committed in the land; the prophets prophesy falsely, and the priests bear rule by their means; and my people love to have it so; and what will ye do in the end thereof?'

The denunciations of this evil are intervolved all through with exhortation, appeal, and promise. The God of fury is a God of reconciliation also, a whirlwind of anger and promise. Man can turn, repent, do well, recognize good as good and evil as evil. It is perhaps natural to the prophets that they should show very little consciousness of the fact that conversion, repentance, and a new life are not the easiest things. They put it, as many saints have done, on almost purely intellectual grounds: 'Come now and let us reason together, saith the Lord'. The lucidity of 'I am that I am' is to be carried into all relations. Surely the thing is clear enough: do this, and all will be well, your sin shall be pardoned. They allow for the fact that people want to sin, but they find it difficult to believe that people do not also want to be intelligent, and since, on their hypothesis, there is no doubt what intelligence involves, they become angry when Israel remains obdurate. That obstinacy in the eyes of the prophets is levelled against something clear and simple, and terrible and complex: a little child leading leopards and lions, lambs and calves, no hurt and no destruction; and peace and the bliss of heaven communicated again in the natural good of earth.

If, however, the obstinate heart is turned, it is to find mercy and pardon. 'I, even I, am he that blotteth out thy transgressions for mine own sake, and will not remember thy sins.' The act of pardon is an act of oblivion. The appeal of the repentant is for the same forgetfulness: be tender, forget the evil, remember the good! In the great prayer of Solomon at the opening of the temple the cry strikes up continually: 'hear thou in heaven thy dwelling-place, and when thou hearest forgive'. Heaven is to be the place and the state of the setting aside of the sin that has been committed. But forgetfulness implies a temporal state; there can be no eternal oblivion of an act of which there is an eternal awareness, and the very nature of eternity is awareness of all: 'the perfect and simultaneous possession of everlasting life'.

The prophets are too much concerned with their demand for penitence and their message of pardon to have time for metaphysics. They allow this anthropomorphism—more serious, because more philosophical—to pass. The fiery and amber likeness of the appearance of a man is not likely to deceive many hearers of Ezekiel, but the idea that the Lord is of time is more dangerous. But Ezekiel and his companions are no more concerned with a metaphysical analysis of the absolute than they are with a defence of the myths of a condescended apparition. They are hammering at the heart. Heaven to them is not so much of eternity as it is of the specious present—the present in which there is time to do things about the past and future, to reason, to repent, to redeem. Yet the reader who, by his detachment or his frowardness, can escape the hammer of their command, the chisel of their entreaty, is left with the problem still in his mind: how can the High and Holy One forget? how can he refuse to know what has been? how can the eternity of heaven exclude from itself the knowledge of man's knowing good in schism, and of good as evil? how can the Lord forgive? In what possible sense can the deeds that are as scarlet be as white as snow, and those that are crimson as wool? And if the indescribable Omnipotence could, then what of man? can he only find felicity by losing fact? It is not conceivable that Omniscience should forget; it is not satisfactory that the redeemed should forget. If a corner of experience is to be hidden, the unity is by so much impaired.

The problem is left unanswered. It has, indeed, only been raised because of the appearance in the heavens of this new quality—say, rather, of this new word. The truth is that the word is not yet defined. We think it is already clear because we impart into it our second-rate meanings. We have some justification. The Lord is presented in effect as saying: 'Well, We will say no more about it'; or (more shockingly): 'Well, We forgive you on condition that you don't do it again'. The condition in these books is a little too obviously prevalent. Blake answered it out of man's heart:

> *Doth Jehovah forgive a debt only on condition that it shall*
> *Be payed? Doth he forgive pollution only on conditions of purity?*
> *That debt is not forgiven! That pollution is not forgiven!*
> *Such is the forgiveness of the gods, the moral virtues of the*
> *Heathen whose tender mercies are cruelty.*

He proceeded to define pardon in another sense; to quote it
would be to import meanings. It is enough here to leave the
word undefined, for if the meaning of pardon (beyond forgetfulness) is obscure, yet the method of the redemption is, to an
extent, comprehensible. There are three principal suggestions.

(1) The first is given most clearly in Jeremiah (xxxi, 33–4)
where the Omnipotence declares that a new contract is to be
made with the inclusive-exclusive thing. It is to be different from
the old contract, which Israel has broken. 'This shall be the
covenant.'

'I will put my law in their inward parts, and write it in their
hearts; and will be their God, and they shall be my people. And
they shall teach no more every man his neighbour, and every
man his brother, saying, Know the Lord: for they shall all know
me, from the least of them unto the greatest of them, saith the
Lord, for I will forgive their iniquity, and I will remember their
sin no more.'

The first point of covenant is the making an inward thing of
the law. It is to be no longer a thing known and obeyed by a
difficult decision; it is to become an instinct, a natural desire of
body and spirit. The doctrine is to be known universally through
the people, so that no one is to teach it or be taught, for all that
remains is the practice, the practice of restored good: 'Ye have
seen . . . how I bore you on eagles' wings and brought you unto
myself . . . ye shall be unto me a kingdom of priests and an holy
nation.' Intercommunication of instinctive good everywhere;
good no more known in any sense as evil; restoration of
humility, of sanctity, of joy.

(2) Nor is the restoration to be limited to Israel; the purpose
of Israel is to be fulfilled through the universal earth. 'The isles
shall wait for his law'; 'my name shall be great among the
Gentiles'. The law that is to be written within is to be written
everywhere: instinctive as the heart, broad as the earth.

(3) All the evil is to be forgotten. Within and without,
present and past, the world is to know good as good, and to
practise it between themselves. There is, however, one group of
passages which, relating to this promise and change, have about

them a difference. They are what are called the Servant Songs of Isaiah. They are generally supposed to consist of the following passages: xlii, 1–4; xlix, 1–6; l, 4–9; lii, 13–liii, 12. They are, of course, regarded now as Messianic, but that is not here the point. There is in them a common element—a figure called 'my servant' or more simply 'He'. This He is the servant and elect of the Lord. He is to be the means of spreading the restoration to the Gentiles (though he is sometimes spoken of as Israel); he is to be, that is, himself an example of the inclusive-exclusive formula. He is as terrible as weapons—swords or arrows; he is to become an astonishment to men; he is to be exalted. But the riddle of his nature reaches its extreme point in the 53rd chapter. There, for the first time, another principle of exchange is hinted. In the early covenant one man was to be responsible for the life of another. Here, however, is another kind of substitution, in the midst of passages of joy and beatitude—'Awake, awake; put on thy strength, O Zion'; 'Sing, O barren, thou that didst not bear'; 'their righteousness is of me, saith the Lord'; 'Ho, every one that thirsteth, come ye to the waters'. This substitution is of a vicarious suffering and success. It is unique in the Old Testament, yet it is in accord with both the law and the promise. It is certainly not here explained.

'For he shall grow up before him as a tender plant, and as a root out of a dry ground: he hath no form nor comeliness; and when we shall see him, there is no beauty that we should desire him.

'He is despised and rejected of men; a man of sorrows, and acquainted with grief: and we hid as it were our faces from him; he was despised, and we esteemed him not.

'Surely he hath borne our griefs, and carried our sorrows: yet we did esteem him stricken, smitten of God, and afflicted.

'But he was wounded for our transgressions, he was bruised for our iniquities: the chastisement of our peace was upon him; and with his stripes we are healed.

'All we like sheep have gone astray; we have turned every one to his own way; and the Lord hath laid on him the iniquity of us all.

He came down from Heaven

'He was oppressed, and he was afflicted, yet he opened not his mouth: he is brought as a lamb to the slaughter, and as a sheep before her shearers is dumb, so he openeth not his mouth.

'He was taken from prison and from judgement: and who shall declare his generation? for he was cut off out of the land of the living: for the transgression of my people was he stricken.'

These then are the main points of the restored life, as far as the prophets know it. The new knowledge is to lose from it the recollection of past sin; it will be remembered neither in heaven nor on earth; the kingdom of the Lord is free from it. The new knowledge again is to be instinctive and natural, a lovely habit, a practice of joy; it will not need instructors and officiants, because all will officiate and instruct; it is to be in the flesh of man and in his heart. It is to expand, by means of Israel, beyond Israel, till it is universal in its effects; a chosen thing is to be its source; and all families of the earth are to be exalted to the same redemption. Last, at least in that single passage, it is to be brought about by some kind of substitution. 'He was oppressed and he was afflicted . . . for the transgression of my people was he stricken.' 'For my thoughts are not your thoughts, neither are your ways my ways, saith the Lord.'

Such is the prophetic movement towards the recovery of that old simple knowledge of good as good; such the promise to the righteous and repentant. It is still a question how sin can be pardoned and in what manner and by what He it can be vicariously borne. But the Old Testament would not be the great book it is if it did not go further on the other side. There is a state of being which discovers, humanly speaking, the monotonous result of man's original choice. It might almost be said that Ecclesiastes represents a state of mind for which the prophets, with their minds set on righteousness, have not allowed. It is, in some sense, a classical expression of utter boredom, though the boredom is set to such high counterpoint that its very expression is exciting. No one who can enjoy Ecclesiastes can be as bored as Ecclesiastes. Indeed, the word is too poor for the grand universality of the meaning. Yet it can hardly be called despair, for if it is despair, it is despair of a particular kind; more like that recorded by the poets at times.

So much I feel my genial spirits droop,
my hopes all flat, nature within me seems
in all her functions weary of herself

My genial spirits fail;
and what can these [the outer world] avail
To lift the smothering weight from off my breast?

It is wan hope, the despair of life itself prolonged through the going-on of life itself, the core of the fruit of the tree of knowledge of good and evil. There is here no immorality; the prophets themselves could hardly complain that Ecclesiastes is hunting after any of the sins they so vehemently denounce. It is possible to relate the book to Solomon in his less moral periods, but that would be to force our own biographical interpretation, like explaining Hamlet by the Earl of Essex, and our own moral, in determining that Ecclesiastes must be wicked because he is bored. In fact, Solomon, or (as it is safer to call him) Ecclesiastes, is not aware of any particular sin. On the contrary, he began by following wisdom, and only when he found that wisdom brought him heaviness of heart did he turn to other methods, with the same result. He has sought out enjoyment and all the great occupations of kings—building, planting, art—and all these labours are a joy for a while, till they fail as wisdom failed. He finds the same thing is true of righteousness itself. The righteous have the reward of the wicked; the wicked have the reward of the righteous. Knowledge of good and knowledge of evil come to the same thing in the end; the second knowledge negatives all; 'there is no profit under the sun'. And there is no other side to the sun; two-dimensioned only, the flat light shines on a flat world from which the third dimension of significance has departed. That lack of significance is sometimes a pleasantness and a joy—even a necessity if we are to enjoy significance at other times, and God must sometimes deign to hide himself. But now it is continual, and therefore has lost all value. A single-

toned universe is unbearable. 'I said that this also is vanity.'
The too-famous refrain closes all activity, and the Canon of the
Bible contains, by the peculiar inspiration of Providence, a complete rejection of life. 'Therefore I hated life; because the work
that is wrought under the sun is grievous unto me: for all is
vanity and vexation of spirit.' And again, more sublimely:
'Whereupon I praised the dead which are already dead more
than the living which are yet alive. Yea, better is he than both
they, which hath not yet been, who hath not seen the evil work
that is done under the sun.' Death is release, for life is worse than
death, and yet also death is worse than life. The living have one
single advantage; they have a hope. 'The living know that they
shall die; but the dead know not anything.' The paradox of
vanity is complete, and the full force of it sinks slowly into the
heart. This is the conclusion of the knowledge of good and evil.
Life, in that first great myth of origin, was given as good, and
man thought it would be fine and godlike to enjoy it also as evil.
This is the result—life is no good and death is no good, and the
most fortunate are those who have not been. For man's nature
is such that he must prefer to live in hope of death than not to
live or hope at all. The single joy of existence is to know that
existence will stop; by so much, and by so much only, existence
is better than non-existence. And then it does stop, and there is
an end; 'man cometh in with vanity, and departeth in darkness'.
Lucretius consoled men for death; 'think—you will not then desire; you will not miss anything, for you will not know of
anything to miss'. That is no satisfaction here.

Along with this decision runs a willing acknowledgement of the
existence of God, and of the will of God towards righteousness.
Ecclesiastes does not object to righteousness; only the end of
righteousness is like the end of everything else. God exists—
certainly; man is to obey him—certainly. But life is unrelated to
this obedience. His conclusion therefore is: 'Remember thy
Creator, and hope to die.' He does not argue with God like Job.
Job desires death, and curses his birth, but he vehemently
demands that God shall explain the whole accursed business.
The docility of Ecclesiastes does not argue or demand; the

result of that too would doubtless be vanity. He accepts all, without delight, without anger, without goodwill. He has rejected life and death, and there is nothing to do but to put up with what comes. But Job had refused to put up with what came, until in the end the Lord himself came, compelled out of the air into the whirlwind of reply by the challenging voice of his creature.

It is true Ecclesiastes does not take immortality into account. The dead, to him, are wholly or entirely dead. But the mere introduction of immortality will not help. There is no reason to suppose that an experience of unending time would be happier than an experience of a brief period of time, unless something else were introduced, and of the introduction of anything else Ecclesiastes has seen no signs. On the contrary, immortality, he thinks, leaves those subject to it worse off by depriving them of their one positive joy—the hope of death. No, 'let us hear the conclusion of the whole matter: Fear God and keep his commandments, for this is the whole duty of man. For God shall bring every work into judgement, with every secret thing.' This, no doubt, is wisdom; and wisdom also is vanity and vexation of spirit.

Such, beyond the prophets, is the undertone of man's knowledge; such is the wise man's judgement. The mystics and the saints desire and demand and promise; the storm of divine anger and divine peace rages from the heavens; an infinite riddle of substitution is sung to the heart of the devout. But Ecclesiastes spoke of what he knew, and of what many millions of others have known after him.

CHAPTER IV

The Precursor and the Incarnation
of the Kingdom

The earliest of the Gospels is asserted to be that called 'of Mark'; it is certainly the shortest. As Genesis had explained what was happening by what had happened, so do the Gospels. They purport to be a record of the cause of certain definite experiences. The time and place of that cause are definitely marked. It occurs in certain named towns of the Roman Empire, in a period from 4 B.C. to A.D. 30, from forty to seventy years after the death of Julius Caesar, and from fifteen to fifty years after the death of Virgil. The administration of the Imperial Government organizes everything, and the events are plotted along the lines of that organization. The *pietas* of the early and mythical wanderers has become a supernatural civilization. The documents of the New Testament are themselves composed in or directed to localities in that interrelated whole, and before it is well understood what the Church is, it is at least clear that it is universal. At the same time, history and contemporaneity again go together, the obverse and the reverse of the coins of the kingdom of heaven. Its missionaries declared a unity, as they do to-day, a unity no more divided by two thousand years than by two seconds. We certainly have to separate them in thought, because of the needs of the mind, as we have sometimes to divide form and content in poetry. But as the poetry is in fact one and indivisible, so is the fact; so even is the doctrine. The thing as it happens on the earth and in the world, the thing as it happens on the earth and in the soul, are two stresses on one fact; say, on one Word. The fact is the thing that is supposed to have appeared, and the Gospel of Mark is the shortest account. The Gospels called 'of Matthew' and 'of Luke' are longer and fuller. The Gospel called 'of John' comes nearer to describing the unity of the new thing in world and soul; it is the limit of the permissible influence of contemporary Greek philosophy, and the repulse of the impermissible. To observe something of the distinction one has only to consider the *Symposium* of Plato with the Gospel of John, and remark the difference in their attitude towards matter.

It is asserted that the Gospel according to Mark was in circulation at Rome by the year 75. If so, and if the Gospel of Mark represents at all what the Church believed or tried to believe in the year 75, then certainly by the year 75 the Church at the centre of a highly developed society had already thrown over any idea (if any such idea had ever existed) of a figure only of brotherly love and international peace; the moral teacher expanding the old Jewish ideas of pardon and righteousness into a fresh beauty, and teaching ethics in the ancient maxim of the Golden Rule. Possibly a figure of this kind might be extracted from Saint John's Gospel, by leaving out rather more than half of Saint John's Gospel. But with the Gospel of Saint Mark the thing is impossible. To remove the apocalyptic is not to leave the ethical but to leave nothing at all.

It is, of course, arguable that the influence of Saint Paul, who is often regarded as the villain of early Christianity (the Claudius of a *Hamlet* from which Hamlet has been removed), had already had its perfect work. Or, since there had not been very much time for Saint Paul to do it, perhaps someone earlier, an Ur-Paul, or (documentarily) the fatal and fascinating Q which no man has seen at any time but the contents of which we so neatly know. The weakness, credulity, and folly of that early disciple, or of all the early disciples, may have altered the original truth of the vagrant provincial professor of ethical beauty into something more closely corresponding to their romantic needs. Saint Mark may be dogmatically asserted to have been an intentional or unintentional liar. But at least we have to admit his lies for the purpose of explaining that they are lies. They are our only evidence for whatever it was he was lying about. And as he was not lying in a sub-prefecture of Thule, but right in the middle of the Empire, so he was not lying about events older than the dynasties of Egypt or the cities of Assyria, but about events done on a hill outside a city on a Roman highway under the rule of the Princeps Augustus and his successor Tiberius. They were (in one sense or the other—or both) historic lies.

Our contemporary pseudo-acquaintance with the Christian idea has misled us in another point. It is generally supposed that his lies (if lies) are simple and easy. It is only by reading Saint Mark that one discovers they are by no means simple or easy. It is very difficult to make out what is supposed to be happening. His book begins with a declaration: 'The beginning of the Gospel of Jesus Christ, the Son of God'. What the Son of God may be he does not explain, preferring to follow it up with a quotation from the old prophets which slides into an account of a certain John who came as the precursor of this Divine Hero. He has in Saint Mark no other business, and this (though highly wrought to a fine passion of declamation and heraldry) is so in Saint John. But in Saint Luke there is something more. It is recorded that certain groups came to the Precursor—the common people, the tax-collectors, the soldiers. All these ask him for some kind of direction on conduct. Saint Matthew adds the ecclesiastical leaders, but the Precursor offered them no more than invective. He answers the rest with instructions which amount very nearly to a gospel of temporal justice. All men are to share their goods freely and equally. The revenue officers are to make no personal profit out of their business. The soldiers are not to make their duties an excuse for outrage or violence; they (again) are to make no personal gain beyond their government pay. Share everything; neither by fraud nor by force let yourself be unfair to anyone; be content with your own proper pay. It is true he does not raise the question of the restoration of the dispossessed by force of arms; he is speaking of immediate duties as between individual and individual. 'He

that has two coats let him give to him that hath none.' He pro-
longs the concern of the prophets with social injustice, without
their denunciation of the proud. That had been declared, as a
duty of the Imperial government, by the great poet dead forty-
five years before:

Pacisque imponere morem,
Parcere subiectis et debellare superbos:

'To impose the habit of peace, to be merciful to the down-
trodden, and to overthrow the proud.' There had been a similar
note in the private song (again according to Saint Luke) of the
Mother of the coming Hero: 'the rich he hath sent empty away'.

At this moment the Divine Thing appears (it will be remembered that Saint Matthew uses the neuter—'that holy *thing*';
students of the Gospel may be excused for sometimes following
the example, if only to remind ourselves of what the Evangelists
actually said). In the rest of Saint Mark's first chapter, the
account of his coming is purely apocalyptic. Witness is borne
out of heaven and on earth and from hell. He (since the masculine
pronoun is also and more frequently used) begins his own activities. He calls disciples; he works miracles of healing; he con-
trols spirits; he teaches with authority. What does he teach?
what do the devils fear and the celestials declare and men wonder
at? 'The time is fulfilled, and the kingdom of God is at hand;
repent ye and believe the gospel.'

Yes, but what gospel? what kind of kingdom? The Precursor
had said almost the same thing. In some expectation one turns the
page . . . several pages. The works of healing continue swiftly,
interspersed with the Divine Thing's comments on himself, and
his reasons for existing. They are still not very clear. The old
prophetic cry of 'pardon' returns. He has power to forgive sins
—does he mean forget? He calls himself the 'Son of Man'; he is
lord of ritual observances such as the keeping of the Sabbath;
there exists some state of eternal sin and damnation. There is
something—presumably the kingdom of heaven—which cannot
be reconciled with old things; new, it must be fitted to the new.

Presently, in the parables, the description of the kingdom is

continued. It is a state of being, but not a state of being without
which one can get along very well. To lose it is to lose everything else. It is intensely dangerous, and yet easily neglected.
It involves repentance and it involves 'faith'—whatever 'faith'
may be. It is concerned with himself, for he attributes to himself
the power and the glory. He says: 'I say unto thee, Arise'; 'it
is I; be not afraid.' The Sermon on the Mount is full of his own
decisions, just as it ramps with hell and destruction and hypo-
crites and being cast into the fire and trodden under foot and
demands for perfection and for joy (not for resignation or en-
durance or forgiveness, not even a pseudo-joy) under intolerable
treatment. Moses in old days had momentarily taken the power
and the glory to himself, and had been shut out of the temporal
promise. But the present Hero does it continuously, until (in
the topmost note of that exalted arrogance) humility itself is
vaunted, and the only virtue that cannot be aware of itself without losing its nature is declared by the Divine Thing to be its
own nature: 'I am meek and lowly of heart.' This in the voice
that says to the Syrophoenician woman when she begs help for
her daughter: 'It is not meet to take the children's bread, and to
cast it unto the dogs.' It is true her request is granted, in answer
to her retort, something in the same manner as the Lord spoke
to Job in answer to his.

About half-way through the book as we have it, there is a
change. Up to Chapter viii it is possible to believe that, though
the doctrine is anything but clear, the experience of the disciples
is not unique. Figures are sometimes met who overwhelm,
frighten, and delight those who come in contact with them;
personality, and so forth—and what they say may easily sound
obscure. But in Chapter viii there is a sudden concentration and
even exposition. The Hero demands from his disciples a statement, not of their repentance or righteousness or belief in the
I AM, which is what the old prophets clamoured for, but of their
belief in himself, and he follows it up with a statement of his own.
They say: 'Thou art the Christ.' No doubt when we have looked
up annotated editions and Biblical dictionaries, we know what
'the Christ' means. It is 'the Anointed One'. But at the moment,

there, it is a kind of incantation, the invocation of a ritual, antique, and magical title. Even if we look up the other Gospels and make it read: 'Thou art the Christ, the Son of the living God,' it does not much help. However inspired Saint Peter may have been, it seems unlikely that he comprehended in a flash the whole complex business of Christian theology. What is the Son of God? The apostles and the devils agree; that is something. But on what do they agree?

The Divine Thing approves the salutation. It proceeds to define its destiny. It declares it is to suffer greatly, to be rejected by all the centres of jurisdiction, to be seized and put to death, and after three days it is to rise again from the dead. Protests are abusively tossed aside. In all three gospels this definition of its immediate future is followed by a definition of its further nature and future; 'the Son of Man' is to be seen in the 'glory of his Father and with the holy angels', that is, in the swift and geometrical glory seen by Isaiah and Ezekiel, the fire of the wheels and the flash of the living creatures, the terrible crystal and the prism of the covenant above, the pattern of heaven declared in heaven. The formula of the knowledge of this pattern on earth is disclosed; it is the loss of life for the saving of life, 'for my sake and the gospel's'. It is the denial of the self and the lifting of the cross.

The denial of the self has come, as is natural, to mean in general the making of the self thoroughly uncomfortable. That (though it may be all that is possible) leaves the self still strongly existing. But the phrase is more intellectual than moral, or rather it is only moral because it is intellectual; it is a denial of the consciousness of the existence of the self at all. What had been the self is to become a single individual, neither less nor more than others; as it were, one of the living creatures that run about and compose the web of the glory. 'Do unto others as you would they should do unto you.' The contemplation demanded is not personal, of the self and of others—even in order that the self may be unselfish—but abstract and impartial. The life of the self is to be lost that the individual soul may be found, in the pattern of the words of the Son of Man. The

51

kingdom is immediately at hand—'Verily I say unto you, That there be some of them that stand here, which shall not taste of death, till they have seen the kingdom of God come with power'; again the words are historic and contemporary at once.

The declaration of the formula is followed by what is called the Transfiguration. Secluded among a few of his followers, the Divine Thing exhibits itself in a sudden brightness, in which, as if it receded into the eternal state of contemporaneousness, the ancient leaders of what had once been the inclusive-exclusive covenant of salvation are discerned to exchange speech with the new exclusive figure of inclusive beatitude. It is a vision which is to be kept a secret till the rising from the dead has been accomplished. But at least the kingdom has now been, to some extent, exhibited. Repentance is a preliminary to the denial of the self and the loss of the life, and the loss of the life for the saving of the life depends on that choosing of necessity by the Son of Man which will take him to his death and rising. 'He set his face to go up to Jerusalem.'

It is at some time during this period of the operation of the Christ that the problem of the Precursor reappears. Messengers from John arrive; 'art thou he that was to come?' After they have been dismissed, the Christ, turning to those that stood by (as it were to his mother and to his brethren), makes the astonishing declaration that 'among men born of women is none greater than John the Baptist, yet the least in the Kingdom of Heaven is greater than he'. The Church since then has implied that this can hardly be true in its literal sense, for the Precursor has been canonized (as it were, by acclamation) and been given a Feast to himself, a Primary Double of the First Class. Even so, even assuming that as a matter of fact the Precursor was and is one of the greatest in the kingdom of heaven, still the Christ must have had something in his mind. What, apart from the expectation of the Redeemer, was the gospel of the Precursor? It was something like complete equality and temporal justice, regarded as the duty of those who expect the kingdom. What has happened to that duty in the gospel of the Kingdom?

The new gospel does not care much about it. All John's

doctrine is less than the least in the Kingdom. It cannot be bothered with telling people not to defraud and not to be violent and to share their superfluities. It tosses all that sort of thing on one side. Let the man who has two coats (said the Precursor) give one to the man who has none. But what if the man who has none, or for that matter the man who has three, wants to take one from the man who has two—what then? Grace of heaven! why, give him both. If a man has stolen the pearl bracelet, why, point out to him that he has missed the diamond necklace. Be content with your wages, said the Precursor. The Holy Thing decorated that advice with a suggestion that it is iniquity to be displeased when others who have done about a tenth as much work are paid as much money: 'is thine eye evil because mine is good?' It is true that there is a reason—those who came in late had not been hired early. No one would accept that as a reason to-day—neither economist nor employer nor worker. But there is always a reason; the intellectual logic of the Prophets is carried on into the New Testament. Yet the separate and suitable reasons never quite account for the identical and indivisible command. The 'sweet reasonableness' of Christ is always there, but it is always in a dance and its dancing-hall is from the topless heavens to the bottomless abyss. Its balance is wholly in itself; it is philosophical and unconditioned by temporalities—'had, having, and in quest to have, extreme'.

Half a hundred brief comments, flung out to the mob of men's hearts, make it impossible for a child of the kingdom, for a Christian, to talk of justice or injustice so far as he personally is concerned; they make it impossible for him to *complain* of the unfairness of anything. They do not, presumably, stop him noticing what has happened, but it can never be a matter of protest. Judgement and measurement are always discouraged. You may have them if you will, but there is a sinister note in the promise that they shall be measured back to you in the same manner: 'good measure, pressed down and running over shall men give into your bosoms'. If you must have law, have it, 'till thou hast paid the uttermost farthing'.

What then of all the great tradition, the freeing of slaves at the Exodus, the determination of the prophets, the long effort against the monstrous impiety of Cain? The answer is obvious; all that is assumed as a mere preliminary. The rich, while they remain rich, are practically incapable of salvation, at which all the Apostles were exceedingly astonished. Their astonishment is exceedingly funny to our vicariously generous minds. But if riches are not supposed to be confined to money, the astonishment becomes more general. There are many who feel that while God might damn Rothschild he could hardly damn Rembrandt. Are the riches of Catullus and Carnegie so unequal, though so different? Sooner or later, nearly everyone is surprised at some kind of rich man being damned. The Divine Thing, for once, was tender to us; he restored a faint hope: 'with God all things are possible'. But the preliminary step is always assumed: 'sell all that thou hast and give it to the poor' —and then we will talk. Then we will talk of that other thing without which even giving to the poor is useless, the thing for which at another time the precious ointment was reserved from the poor, the thing that is necessary to correct and qualify even good deeds, the thing that is formulated in the words 'for my sake and the gospel's' or 'in my name'. Good deeds are not enough; even love is not enough unless it is love of a particular kind. Long afterwards Saint Paul caught up the dreadful cry: 'though I bestow all my goods to feed the poor . . . and have not charity, it profiteth me nothing'. It is not surprising that Messias saw the possibility of an infinitely greater knowledge of evil existing through him than had been before: 'blessed is he whosoever shall not be offended at me'.

The Incarnation of the Kingdom has declared its destiny, the formula by which man may be unified with it, the preliminaries necessary to the spiritual initiation. The records of the Synoptics proceed to the awful and familiar tale: to the entry of the Divine Thing into Jerusalem, to its making of itself a substance of communication through the flesh, to its Passion. 'The Son of Man is betrayed into the hands of sinners.' In the ancient myth something of that kind had happened to the good, the good in which the Adam had lived. But that good had not, in the myth, been imagined as a consciousness. The kingdom of heaven then had not been shown as affected by the sin of the Adam; only the Adam. The patience which had been proclaimed in the covenants had been the self-restraint of the Creator, but not—there—of the Victim. Another side of the aeonian process has issued slowly into knowledge; the operation of that in the Adam and in their descendants which had remained everlastingly related to the good.

The Gospel called 'of John' begins with that original. The Divine Thing is there identified with the knowledge of good which indefectibly exists in every man—indefectibly even though it should be experienced only as hell—'the light which lighteth every man'. It is also that by which communication with the heaven of perfection is maintained, 'ascending and descending'. But this state of being which is called 'the kingdom of heaven' in the Synoptics is called in Saint John 'eternal life'. There is no space here to work out singly the various definitions of itself which it provides in this Gospel. Briefly, it declares itself to be the union of heaven and earth (i, 51); the one absolutely necessary thing for escape from a state in which the contradiction of good is preferred (iii, 16, 36); it is the perfect satisfaction of desire (vi, 35; x, 27–8); it is judgement (v, 25–30; xii, 46–8); it is in perfect union with its Origin (x, 30; xiv, 11); it is universal and inclusive (xv, 5; xvii, 21); it restores the truth (v, 33; vii, 31–2; xviii, 37). Of these the last is perhaps the most related to the present argument. For by truth must be meant at least perfect knowledge (within the proper requisite degrees). 'Ye shall know the truth, and the truth shall make you free.' Right knowledge and freedom are to be one.

It is this 'truth' of which the Divine Hero speaks at the time of the Passion which he had prophesied—as necessity and as his free choice. Before one of the jurisdictions by which he is rejected and condemned he declares: 'To this end was I born, and for this cause came I into the world, that I should bear witness unto the truth. Everyone that is of the truth heareth my voice'. He formally claimed before another the ritual titles of Son of

He came down from Heaven

God and Son of Man, and his future descent 'in the clouds of heaven' and in the glory of heaven. But before then the earlier proclamation, 'the kingdom of heaven is at hand', has changed. It has become concentrated; if the kingdom, then the moment of the arrival of the kingdom. The Gospels break into peremptory phrases: 'My time is at hand', 'this night', 'this hour'; an image of the hour absorbed into the Holy Thing is thrown up— 'this cup'; the hour arrives—'behold, the Son of Man is betrayed into the hands of sinners'.

Around that moment the world of order and judgement, of Virgil and the Precursor, of Pharaoh and Cain, rushes up also. Its good and its evil are both concerned, for it cannot very well do other than it does do. The knowledge of good as evil has made the whole good evil to it; it has to reject the good in order to follow all that it can understand as good. When Caiaphas said that 'it was good that one man should die for the people', he laid down a principle which every government supports and must support. Nor, though Christ has denounced the government for its other sins, does he denounce either Caiaphas or Pilate for his own death. He answers the priest; he condescends to discussion with the Roman. Only to Herod he says nothing, for Herod desired neither the ecclesiastical nor the political good; he wanted only miracles to amuse him. The miracles of Christ are accidental, however efficient; the kingdom of heaven fulfils all earthly laws because that is its nature but it is concerned only with its own, and to try to use it for earth is to lose heaven and gain nothing for earth. It may be taken by violence but it cannot be compelled by violence; its Incarnation commanded that he should be awaited everywhere but his effectiveness demanded nowhere. Everything must be made ready and then he will do what he likes. This maxim, which is the condition of all prayer, has involved the Church in a metaphysic of prayer equivalent to 'Heads, I win; tails, you lose'.

The three jurisdictions acted according to all they could understand of good: Caiaphas upon all he could know of the religious law, Pilate of the Virgilian equity, Herod of personal desire. The Messias answered them in that first word of the

Cross which entreated pardon for them precisely on the ground of their ignorance: 'forgive them, for they know not what they do'. The knowledge of good and evil which man had desired is offered as the excuse for their false knowledge of good. But the offer brings their false knowledge into consciousness, and will no longer like the prophets blot it out. The new way of pardon is to be different from the old, for the evil is still to be known. It is known, in what follows, by the Thing that has come down from Heaven. He experiences a complete and utter deprivation of all knowledge of the good. The Church has never defined the Atonement. It has contented itself with saying that the Person of the kingdom there assumed into itself the utmost possible capacities of its own destruction and they could not destroy it. It separated itself from all good deliberately and (as it were) superfluously: 'thinkest thou I cannot now pray to the Father and he shall presently give me more than twelve legions of angels? But how then shall the scriptures be fulfilled, that thus it must be?' It could, it seems, still guiltlessly free itself, but it has made its own promise and will keep it. Its impotency is deliberate. It denies its self; it loses its life to save it; it saves others because it cannot, by its decisions, save itself. It remains still exclusive and inclusive; it excludes all consent to the knowledge of evil, but it includes the whole knowledge of evil without its own consent. It is 'made sin', in Saint Paul's phrase. The prophecy quoted concerning this paradox of redemption is 'A bone of him shall not be broken', and this is fulfilled; as if the frame of the universe remains entire, but its life is drawn out of it, as if the pattern of the glory remained exact but the glory itself were drawn away. The height of the process begins with the Agony in the Garden, which is often quoted for our encouragement; he shuddered and shrank. The shrinking is part of the necessity; he 'must' lose power; he 'must' know fear. He 'must' be like the Adam in the garden of the myth, only where they fled from their fear into the trees he goes among the trees to find his fear; he is secluded into terror. The process reaches its height, after from the cross he has still asserted the *pietas*, the exchanged human responsibility, of men: 'behold thy son, behold thy mother', and after he has still declared the pure dogma of his nature, known now as hardly more than dogma: 'to-day thou shalt be with me in Paradise'. This is what he has chosen, and as his power leaves him he still chooses, to believe. He becomes, but for that belief, a state wholly abandoned.

Gibbon, in that superb as well as solemn sneer which is one of the classic pages of English prose as well as one of the supreme attacks on the whole history, may have been right. The whole earth may not have been darkened, nor even the whole land. Pliny and Seneca may have recorded no wonder because there was no wonder to record. The sun may have seemed to shine on Calvary as on many another more protracted agony. Or there may have been a local eclipse, or whatever other phenomenon the romantic pietists can invent to reconcile themselves to the other side. But that the life of the whole of mankind began to fail in that hour is not incredible; that the sun and all light, without as within, darkened before men's eyes, that the swoon of something more than death touched them, and its sweat stood on their foreheads to the farthest ends of the world. The Thing that was, and had always been, and must always be; the fundamental humanity of all men; the Thing that was man rather than a man, though certainly incarnated into the physical appearance of a man; the Thing that was Christ Jesus, knew all things in the deprivation of all goodness.

The darkness passed; men went on their affairs. He said: 'It is finished.' The Passion and the Resurrection have been necessarily divided in ritual and we think of them as separate events. So certainly they were, and yet not as separate as all that. They are two operations in one; they are the hour of the coming of the kingdom. A new knowledge arises. Men had determined to know good as evil; there could be but one perfect remedy for that—to know the evil of the past itself as good, and to be free from the necessity of the knowledge of evil in the future; to find right knowledge and perfect freedom together; to know all things as occasions of love. The Adam and their children had been involved in a state of contradiction within themselves. The law had done its best by imposing on that chaos of contradiction a kind of order, by at least calling definite things good and definite things evil. The prophets had urged this method: repent, 'cease to do evil, learn to do well'. But even allowing that, in all times and places, it was possible to know what was good and what was evil, was it as easy as all that? Or what of Job who had done well and was overthrown? Or Ecclesiastes who had sought out righteousness and found it was all much the same vanity in the end? How could the single knowledge be restored? Or if the myth itself were false, how could the single knowledge be gained—the knowledge of perfection in all experience which man naturally desires and naturally believes, and as naturally denies and contradicts?

The writings of the early masters of the new life, the life that was declared after the Resurrection, are full of an awful simplicity. The thing has happened; the kingdom is here. 'Fear not, little flock,' wrote one of them, 'it is your Father's good pleasure to give you the kingdom.' 'What shall deliver me', wrote another, 'from the body of this death? I thank God, through Jesus Christ our Lord.' This clarity of knowledge rides through the Epistles. All is most well; evil is 'pardoned'—it is known after another manner; in an interchange of love, as a means of love, therefore as a means of the good. *O felix culpa*— pardon is no longer an oblivion but an increased knowledge, a knowledge of all things in a perfection of joy.

It is the name now given to the heavenly knowledge of the evil of earth; evil is known as an occasion of good, that is, of love. It has been always so known on the side of heaven, but now it can be so known on the side of earth also. Pardon, or reconciliation, was not defined by the prophets as more than oblivion, for in time mankind had not experienced that reconciliation. Nor could mankind, by itself, ever reach it, for mankind by itself could not endure the results of its choice, the total deprivation of good, and yet recover joyous awareness of good. What mankind could not do, manhood did, and a manhood which was at the disposal of all men and women. It was therefore possible now for mankind itself to know evil as an occasion of heavenly love. It was not inappropriate that the condition of such a pardon should be repentance, for repentance is no more than a passionate intention to know all things after the mode of heaven, and it is impossible to know evil as good if you insist on knowing it as evil. Pardon, as between any two beings, is a reidentification of love, and it is known so in the most tender and the most happy human relationships. But there is a profound difference between any such reidentification of love between heaven and earth and between earth and earth. What may be justly required in the one case must not be required in the other. It is all very well for the Divine Thing of heaven to require some kind of intention of good, not exactly as a condition of pardon but as a means of the existence of its perfection. Men were never meant to be as gods or to know as gods, and for men to make any such intention a part of their pardon is precisely to try to behave as gods. It is the renewal of the first and most dreadful error, the desire to know as gods; the reversal of the Incarnation, by which God knew as Man, the heresy of thought and action denounced in the Athanasian Creed—it is precisely the attempt to convert the Godhead into flesh and not the taking of the manhood into God. The intention to do differently may be passionately offered; it must never be required—not in the most secret recesses of that self which can only blush with shame to find itself pardoning and with delight at the infinite laughter of the universe at a created being forgiving another created being. The ancient cry of 'Don't do it again' is never a part of pardon. It is conceivable that Saint Peter reidentified love between himself and his brother four hundred and ninety times in a day; it is inconceivable that each time he made it a condition of love that it shouldn't happen again—it would be a slur on intelligence as well as love. To consent to know evil as good only on condition that the evil never happens again is silly; it is conditioning one's knowledge—as if one consented to know that the Antipodes existed only on condition that no one ever mentioned the Antipodes. All limitation of pardon must come, if at all, from the side of the sinner, in the frequent cry of 'I won't do it again', in the more frequent cry of 'I won't, but I shall. . . .' Heaven has had to explain to us not only itself but ourselves; it has had to

60

create for us not only pardon but the nature of the desire for pardon. It has therefore defined the cry of the sinner, but it has not suggested that other sinners should take upon themselves to demand the cry before they submit, with their brothers, to its single glorious existence in both.

He rose; he manifested; he talked of 'the things pertaining to the kingdom'. He exhibited the actuality of his body, carrying the lovely and adorable matter, with which all souls were everlastingly conjoined, into his eternity. He left one great commandment—satisfy hunger: 'feed the lambs', 'feed the sheep'. Beyond the Petrine law he cast the Johannine—'if I will that he tarry till I come . . .' but the coming may be from moment to moment and the tarrying from moment to moment. 'Jesus said not unto him, He shall not die; but, If I will that he tarry till I come, what is that to thee?' It is as if, from moment to moment, he withdrew and returned, swifter than lightning, known in one mode and another mode and always new. The new life might still be sequential (in the order of time) but every instant was united to the Origin, and complete and absolute in itself. 'Behold, I come quickly'—the coming and the going one, the going and the coming one, and all is joy. 'It is not for you to know the times and the seasons . . . but you shall be witnesses to me . . . to the uttermost ends of the earth', through all the distances and all the operations of holy matter.

Then, as if it withdrew into the air within the air, and the air became a cloud about its passage, scattering promises of power, the Divine Thing parted and passed.

CHAPTER V

The Theology of Romantic Love

There are', wrote Wordsworth,

> *There are in our existence spots of time,*
> *That with distinct pre-eminence retain*
> *A renovating virtue, whence, depressed*
> *By false opinion and contentious thought,*
> *Or aught of heavier or more deadly weight,*
> *In trivial occupations, and the round*
> *Of ordinary intercourse, our minds*
> *Are nourished and invisibly repaired.*

It is these pre-eminent and renovating moments which differ
in different civilizations and philosophies. Life itself is much of a
muchness wherever it is lived, but our efforts to draw the muchness (in the Dormouse's phrase) change. It may not make much
difference, as that other great creature, Dr. Johnson, who had so
much in common with the figures of Alice's Wonderland, told
Boswell, under what government a man lives. But the kind of
philosophy under which he lives does make a little, by means of
the pre-eminent moments. Those moments are often interpreted
in terms of the then dominant philosophy, but they retain their
richness, and (at least for a while) they enrich the philosophy.
An exchange takes place between ideas and events, and that
exchange is communicated, at those moments, first to the more
creative and afterwards to all minds.

In the centuries after the passing of Christ there grew up in
Europe a great metaphysical civilization, a society as much based
on a philosophical principle as the first Roman Empire had been

on the evasion of philosophical principles. The fundamental idea was salvation. The grand substitution had been, and was being, carried out, and society was to be organized on the basis of a belief in substitution and salvation. It had, of course, many other elements; it had something of the Precursor, and a very great deal of Pharaoh, but it thought in terms of the Apostles. The celebration of the Mass did not so much prolong the Sacrifice in time as turn time back to the Sacrifice; communion mystically united the pious to heaven and the impious to hell; the ceremony of penance was instituted to spread everywhere the public news of a secret pardon. To the naturally outstanding figures of kings, conquerors, law-givers, and even poets, were now added the supernaturally outstanding figures of those who, by a passion of courtesy towards God and man, seemed even on earth to have fully lost their own lives and attained some other. Experience underwent new interpretation. The Revolution, which had been assumed by Christ as a preliminary to the Kingdom, became entangled with the principles of the Church, and has (to the irritation of both groups of minds) remained somewhat entangled. The Revolution may exist without any demand for the Church, but the Church has never existed long anywhere without creating a demand for a Revolution. 'The poor ye have always with you', said Christ, and wherever his tradition has gone we have been made acutely aware of them. The idea of social justice became important. The idea of tragedy lost its importance—almost its nature. In this world all was, in the end, under Providence, however detestable the enemies of Providence; as when, in one of his loveliest passages, Dante speaks of Luck as being one of the primal creatures, who for ever enjoys her own beatitude, while fools blaspheme her below. Nor could the other world be tragic, since there could hardly be tragedy, whatever grief, in a man's obstinate determination to be damned. So Death at once gained and lost; it gained in frightfulness and in beauty; it lost the profound solace of Lucretius, for immortality (whether a boon or a curse) was now a fact, and final oblivion was forbidden to comfort man's mind. All these alterations filled men's pre-eminent moments with new nourishment and new repair. The imagination of the world and of heaven had changed.

Of all these alterations one affected perhaps more than all the rest (except for the central dogmas) the casual fancies and ordinary outlook of men and women. As a historic fact the change has been described in words better than any I could find by Mr. C. S. Lewis, in one of the most important critical books of our time, *The Allegory of Love*. I may therefore quote him at some length:

'. . . It seems to us natural that love should be the commonest theme of serious imaginative literature: but a glance at classical antiquity or at the Dark Ages at once shows us that what we took for "nature" is really a special state of affairs, which will probably have an end, and which certainly had a beginning in eleventh-century Provence. It seems—or it seemed to us till lately—a natural thing that love (under certain conditions) should be regarded as a noble and ennobling passion: it is only if we imagine ourselves trying to explain this doctrine to Aristotle, Virgil, Saint Paul, or the author of *Beowulf*, that we become aware how far from natural it is.'

'. . . French poets, in the eleventh century, discovered or invented, or were the first to express, that romantic species of passion which English poets were still writing about in the nineteenth. They effected a change which has left no corner of our ethics, our imagination, or our daily life untouched, and they erected impassable barriers between us and the classical past or the Oriental present. Compared with this revolution the Renaissance is a mere ripple on the surface of literature.'

'. . . The new thing itself I do not pretend to explain. Real changes in human sentiment are very rare—there are perhaps three or four on record—but I believe that they occur, and that this is one of them.'

There entered into the relations between the sexes a philosophical, even a religious, idea.[1] That idea had a very long life

[1] I am aware that in the Middle Ages this idea involved conventionally certain conditions, but since they are not of its intellectual essence they need not be here considered.

before it, and was to undergo many unfortunate and fortunate chances. On the one hand, like many other religious ideas, it was to become a superstition; on the other hand, it was to be, naturally but regrettably, cold-shouldered by the ecclesiastical authorities. It was to be an indulgence to the populace and a stumbling-block to the Puritans—using both words of intellectual states of mind. It was to save and endanger souls. And it is still quite uncertain what will happen to it. It may utterly disappear from the earth. But if not, the popular idea of it will probably have to undergo a good deal of purification. In fact, and in itself, it is a thing not of superstition and indulgence, but of doctrine and duty, and not of achievement but of promise.

The pre-eminent moment of romantic love is not, of course, confined to the moment of romantic sex love. There are other moments of intense experience combined with potentiality of further experience. Great art has it and politics and nature and (it is said) maturity. But few of these have had the same universality and few, owing to the chance of genius, have undergone the same analysis. Wordsworth began the task of the analysis of man's experience of nature as a precursor and means to something greater, but for various reasons he left it unfinished. Nature, until recently, had become as much of a superstition as romantic love; it looks, however, as if it would have a shorter period of influence.

The difficulty in any discussion of such experiences is in the finding common ground for discussion. There is no accepted agreement upon what the state which our grandfathers used to call 'falling in love' involves. It is neither sex appetite pure and simple; nor, on the other hand, is it necessarily related to marriage. It is something like a state of adoration, and it has been expressed, of course, by the poets better than by anyone else. Perhaps, therefore, the most convenient way of defining it will be to take a quotation from one of them, and that not from any of the more extreme Romantics but from Milton (who has long enough been regarded as both pious and puritanical). It has here the additional advantage of being imagined as spoken by Adam of Eve, and therefore as an imagined expression of that

E

state of the good in which, before the Fall, they existed. It comes from *Paradise Lost*, Book viii, 546–59:

> . . . *when I approach*
> *Her loveliness, so absolute she seems*
> *And in herself complete, so well to know*
> *Her own, that what she wills to do or say*
> *Seems wisest, virtuousest, discreetest, best.*
> *All higher knowledge in her presence falls*
> *Degraded: Wisdom in discourse with her*
> *Loses, discount'nanced, and like Folly shows:*
> *Authority and Reason on her wait,*
> *As one intended first, not after made*
> *Occasionally: and, to consummate all,*
> *Greatness of mind and nobleness their seat*
> *Build in her loveliest, and create an awe*
> *About her, as a guard angelic placed.*

This then is the contemplation of the object of love from a state of romantic love. There has been and is, now as always, only one question about this state of things: is it serious? is it capable of intellectual treatment? is it capable of belief, labour, fruition? is it (in some sense or other) *true*? It is, of course, true to Adam if the vision has so appeared to him. It was certainly a vision, to Adam, and in the poem, of something like the kingdom of heaven on earth; Eve is at once an inhabitant of the kingdom and the means by which the kingdom is seen. Can this state of things be treated as the first matter of a great experiment? and if so, what exactly is the material? and what exactly are the best conditions of the experiment? The end, of course, is known by definition of the kingdom: it is the establishment of a state of *caritas*, of pure love, the mode of expansion of one moment into eternity. It is, in fact, another example of the operation of the inclusive-exclusive thing; only in this case it is Adam, in the poem, and we, outside the poem, who are expected to do something about it.

There was, in the history of Christendom, a genius of the greatest power whose imagination worked on this theme, and that was Dante. The range of his whole work provides a complete account of the making of the experiment and of its success. It is not, of course, the only theme in Dante: *tot homini quot Dantes*. But at least it is one, and it happens to be one which he very consciously asserted. We shall not therefore be ingeniously extracting a gospel from him of which he knew nothing if we believe him. (There used certainly to be some critics who maintained that there never was a girl in Dante's life at all; at least, any denial of Beatrice must mean this or it means nothing. Once let any girl in—including Gemma Donati—and the principle has been admitted, and only the details can be discussed.) It is not possible here to make any effort to trace the whole philosophical journey. All that can be done is to take, because it is done so much better than we can do it, an analysis here and there. The journey begins in the *New Life* with the first meeting with Beatrice at the age of nine, and with the second meeting at the age of eighteen. It proceeds through every kind of concern until it ends, at almost the close of the *Comedy*, with a state in which those first Beatrician encounters, which were once full of such a thrilling *tremendum*, seem almost paltry, except that they were the beginning of all, compared to the massive whole of single and exchanged Love. In reaching the end, we reach (as in all poetry) the beginning also; the *New Life*, like the *Hell* and the *Purgatory*, exists only by, in, and for the *Paradise* that includes them.

The description of the Beatrician encounters is in the *New Life*. A more intellectual and analytical definition is in the *Banquet*. It is true that it there occurs because of another lady, the 'Lady of the Window', but that does not alter the definitions. The great love poets may have been monogamic in the sense of having one lady at a time; it cannot be said that they had one lady all the time. Nor indeed can it very easily be maintained that Dante was a striking example of New Testament monogamy, considering the extent to which his imagination concentrated itself on one woman while he was married to another. It is part of the incredible irony of the kingdom of heaven that it should produce the most stupendous and scientific statement of the experiment from a poet whom the stricter moralists of the experiment are compelled to disavow or to disguise.

The experience of romantic love then is described in the *New Life* and analysed in the *Banquet*. The intellect is always called on to do its part. The appearance of Beatrice and her image is of so noble a virtue that 'at no time it suffered Love to rule over me without the faithful council of Reason in things where such council was useful'. The first appearance of Beatrice produces three separate effects: it moves the heart as the seat of spiritual emotions, the brain as the centre of perception, and the liver as the place of corporal emotions. It is much to be wished that English literature had kept liver as well as heart; we have to use one word for both emotional states—what (reverting to the old ambiguity of heaven) we might call the spiritual and the spatial heaven of romantic love. Dante did his part in describing the spatial heavens, but it is the spiritual which are here the concern. The following points may be briefly noted (they are taken from sections 3–8 of the third Treatise of the *Convivo*; the translation is from W. W. Jackson's version published by the Clarendon Press).

(1) The intellect 'in discoursing of her, many times wished to infer things about her, though I could not understand them'. The experience—the sight, that is, of the beloved—arouses a sense of intense significance, a sense that an explanation of the whole universe is being offered, and indeed in some sense understood; only it cannot yet be defined. Even when the intellect seems to apprehend, it cannot express its purpose; 'the tongue cannot follow that which the intellect sees'.

(2) 'She is . . . the pattern of man's essence existing in thought within the divine mind . . . she is as completely perfect as the essence of man can possibly be.' She is, that is, the perfect centre and norm of humanity; others exist, it seems, because and in so far as, they resemble her virtue. The extraordinary vision is that of the ordinary thing *in excelsis*.

(3) '. . . The experiences which may be had of her in these operations which are peculiar to the rational soul, into which the divine light radiates with less hindrance, I mean in speech and in

the acts which may be called behaviour and carriage.' It is a convention of love-poetry to speak of light emanating from the person of the beloved; the dichotomy of metaphysics is between those who believe that it does and those who do not. This does not seem to be arguable. The forehead and the hand are radiant; she disseminates glory. Or they do not, and she does not; if it seems so, it does but seem. But no lover was ever content to allow that it was but a seeming; rather, it is to be that portion of the divine light which, in the eternal creation of her in heaven, possesses her. 'The light that lightens every man that comes into the world' is made visible through her, by the will of grace, and by that alone. It seems that no one yet discovered that light of glory in any woman or any man by hunting for it; it seems that it may exist where it is not wanted. It has its own methods; 'my ways are not your ways, saith the Lord'. It is not of a nature certainly to rival the electric light, but whether that is due to its weakness or to the lover's imperfection is another matter. The schools are divided.

(4) 'This lady is a thing visibly miraculous, of which the eyes of men may daily have experience, and this marvel makes all others possible in our eyes . . . this lady with her wondrous aspect assists our faith. Therefore was she from eternity so ordained.' By 'faith' there Dante means faith in 'Him who was crucified'—but then to Dante He who was crucified was a thing natural and fundamental, and not odd and all religious. It is perhaps rather the word 'eternity' which is here suggestive. She appears with this quality, as of something unaffected by time; it is the metaphysical association of the visible light. She is the substance of spirit.

(5) 'I affirm, therefore, that, since we have now ascertained the meaning of this section in which this lady is extolled with regard to her soul, one must now go on to perceive how . . . I extol her with regard to her body. And I say that in her aspect things appear which reveal "some of the joys" (among the many other joys) of Paradise. The noblest pleasure . . . is to feel content, and this is the same as to be blest; and this pleasure, although in a different way, is truly found in the aspect of this

lady . . . with much pleasure does her beauty feed the eyes of those who behold her. But this contentment is different in kind from that felt in Paradise, which is everlasting; for this everlasting contentment cannot fall to anyone here.' The two places where the beauty of the soul most chiefly appears are the eyes and the mouth, and it is the integrity and modesty of the lady that are there mostly to be admired; one may say, the right proportion of candour and restraint, the perfect balance of virtue, opposed yet coexistent.

(6) Her beauty 'surpasses our intellect' 'as the sun surpasses weak sight, not indeed that which is healthy and strong'. The weak sight of the mind cannot properly contemplate this beauty, for 'after gazing freely on it, the soul becomes intoxicated, so that she goes astray in all her operations'. This saying is reminiscent of Messias: 'blessed is he whosoever shall not be offended at me', to whom I am not a cause of greater evil. The glory is apt to dazzle the beholder unless he already has a mind disposed to examine the pattern of the glory. It is more important to do the work of the kingdom than to say 'Lord, Lord'. Indeed, it is by some such going astray that the theology of Romantic Love has been neglected in favour of the superstitions and fables. The effort after the pattern marks the difference. The superstitions make heaven and earth in the form of the beloved; the theology declares that the beloved is the first preparatory form of heaven and earth. Its controlling maxim is that these things are first seen through Beatrice as a means; the corollary is that they are found through Beatrice as a first means only. The preposition refers not only to sight but to progress. For

(7) 'Her beauty has power to renovate nature in those who behold her, which is a marvellous thing. And this confirms what has been said . . . that she is the helper of our faith.' This is perhaps the most profound, most universal, and most widely confirmed saying of all. It is the Dantean equivalent of all the resolutions and reformations rashly attributed to the influence of the beloved. It is also the Dantean equivalent of the first coming of the kingdom. He says, soon after: 'She was created not only to make a good thing better, but also to turn a bad thing into

70

good.' Things intolerable outside a state of love become blessed within: laughter and love convert for a moment the dark habitations within the soul to renewed gardens in Eden. The primal knowledge is restored, and something like pardon restores something like innocence. The 'new life' exists. It cannot continue to exist permanently without faith and labour. Nothing that comes down from heaven can. But it renews nature if only for a moment; it flashes for a moment into the lover the life he was meant to possess instead of his own by the exposition in her of the life she was meant to possess instead of her own. They are 'in love'.

(8) 'This is she who maketh humble all the self-willed; she was the thought of him who set the universe in motion.' She is the phenomenon of the centre; and the chief grace she bestows is humility—the self-forgetfulness which (only) makes room for adoration. She is the vision of the divine glory and the means of the divine grace, and she herself is irresponsible for it and almost irrelevant to it. She is the Mother of Love—of *caritas*, and even of a *caritas* beyond any *caritas* we can imagine; she is the chosen Mother of the goodwill of God.

These then are certain of the definitions which Dante gives of the effect of the appearance of Beatrice. It must be left to any reader to decide how far they form—at least partially—a correct account of a young man in the state of having 'fallen in love'. *Mutatis mutandis*, they may apply to the woman; though, since she is not in Dante, it is rather to Milton's Eve that we must go for a description of her. It is a not unpleasant thought that the word Fall occurs in this experience also; as if the divine grace, after man had insisted on falling once into a divided and contradictory knowledge, had arranged itself to trick him into an unexpected fall into restored and single knowledge. The inclusive-exclusive is a marked sign here of the means of salvation. Eve, Beatrice, or whoever, is certainly her peculiar and (in vision) indefectible self. But she is also the ordinary girl exalted into this extraordinary; she is the norm of all ladies, even if the others do not seem (in the lover's vision) to reach it. The union of flesh and spirit, visible in her (or him), is credible everywhere; indeed, that union, which so much poetry has desired to describe,

71

is understood as more profound and more natural than the dichotomy, of experience or of expression, which has separated them. She is inclusive of both, and exclusive of their separateness. She is, in a final paradox, inclusive even of moments when she is none of these things, and the grace of that state is not least revealed when it excludes itself, as it were, and includes a happy and temporary ignorance of glory in favour of contented play.

The *New Life* had already personified the definitions of the *Banquet*. In the earlier book Beatrice is presented as having on Dante the effect which the *Banquet* analyses. She exists (actual or not, but preferably, on the mere evidence, actual) as a form incarnating what is only afterwards understood as 'the idea or abstraction of its kind'. She meets him, and he her, in the activities of the city; ordinary things happen, and two extraordinary —for she snubs him, and she dies. Two or three incidents bear on the idea of her relation to God. The first is the moment when the girl comes down the street and says 'Good morning' in passing. This thrilling and universal moment is known as 'the salutation of Beatrice'. So, of course, it is, and it is as serious (but not as artistic) as that. It is the flash of the moment in a word. Dante says: 'I say that when she appeared from any place, there was through my hope of her admirable salutation, no enemy remaining to me, but a flame of *caritas* possessed me, which made me pardon anyone who had offended me; and if anyone had then asked me concerning anything, my answer would have been only *Love*, with a face clothed in humility.' Or more colloquially: 'I say that when she came along, I was so thrilled with the mere hope that she would notice me that I was friends with everyone, and utterly full of goodwill, and I was ready to forgive anyone who had offended me. If I had been asked any question at all I should have answered quite humbly *Love*.' The pardon is not a cold superior thing but inevitably produced by *una fiamma di caritade*, a leaping momentary fire of pure love, like the fiery heavenly creatures of Ezekiel. It is accompanied by a communication of humility, as from the source, i.e. that kingdom of heaven which declared in a paradox of divine vitality: 'I am meek and lowly of heart.' Dante does not suggest that he has already achieved a state of humility and pure love; the whole point is that they are unusually summoned up in him by the girl's greeting. To discover the method by which they become habitual and essential is the aim of the grand experiment, and was at least one of the themes of his imagination; to find the point of change of stress, and therefore of significance, so that at the end of the *Comedy* Beatrice properly turns her eyes away from him.

> *Così orai; ed ella sì lontana,*
> *come parea, sorrise e riguardommi;*
> *poi si tornò all'eterna fontana.*

> Thus I prayed; seeming so far,
> she smiled and she gazed back,
> then turned to the eternal spring.

Dante does similarly; he begins to lose consciousness even of her as the full immingled zones of beatitude open; the early refusal of the salutation which had been 'the loss of my beatitude' and an agony is now the very pulse of the final exaltation. In what sense, if ever, Beatrice looks at him again is a thing for consideration only in a more detailed study of the *Comedy*, from the other end of the Paradise.

The second incident is more allegorical, but the allegory is almost a symbolism; that is, it has almost not a likeness but an identity. Dante one day sees another young woman coming along. The whole of the *New Life* is full of other young women, but, whatever they may have been in his life, they are in his imagination part of the inclusiveness of the exclusive thing; they are very necessary and quite unimportant—what one might call a general sex-awareness without credibility. This one is the lover of one of his friends; her name is Giovanna or Joan; she is so lovely that she has been nicknamed Primavera or Spring. Beatrice was coming at a little distance behind. Love then said to Dante: 'If you consider her first name, it is as much as to say *Primavera*, for her name Giovanna is from that Giovanni which preceded the true light, saying: "I am the voice of one crying in

73

the wilderness. Prepare the way of the Lord" . . . He who is willing to consider with subtlety would call Beatrice Love, for the great similarity she has to me.' It would be perhaps unsafe to do so; if by Love is meant the passion of goodwill and humility. But it would be safe to call her the Mother of Love in the soul. The comparison of Giovanna with the Precursor, with that John who preceded '*la verace luce*', makes her the precursor of the divine light which in Beatrice radiates, as was said in the *Banquet*, 'with less hindrance'. The Divine Thing of goodwill and humility which Dante had experienced springs from his experience of Beatrice; she is the Mother of the grace, and even therefore of the occult God. It is a result of the Incarnation that opened all potentialities of the knowledge of the kingdom of heaven in and through matter. 'My covenant shall be in your flesh.'

The third point can only be mentioned; it is the death of Beatrice. No doubt, of Beatrice, assuming Beatrice; the fact need not be denied because it means a great deal more than itself. For nothing seems to be more certain than that the original glory, the *Beatricianness* of Beatrice, does either disappear or at least modify itself. In this also we have an exclusive-inclusive event. Beatrice dies; that is the exclusive. The light and beatitude disappear; that is the inclusive. In the imagination the two need not be hostile, nor in fact. 'The City is widowed', says Dante, quoting Jeremiah. It is apt to be a blow.

When she returns she comes as a judgement. But also her own nature is more particularly declared. It is declared in a very different kind of poem. But what is declared there is in accord with all that had gone before. The first encounter with Beatrice had awakened physical, mental, and spiritual awareness; later encounters had communicated to Dante moments of humility and pure love, however far he might be from staying in them; she had followed Giovanna as Christ followed John. And she dies, and things happen, and this and the other interferes, and Dante in imagination comes to himself in a savage wood, at the foot of a great hill. The hill is 'the cause and occasion of all joy'. He tries to climb; he is driven back by the whole of human life understood in its three great images of the gay and beautiful Leopard of youth, the strong and haughty Lion of middle-age, and the terrible insatiable Wolf of old age. These which make up Time, or make up at least all of Time that matters to Dante, drive him back from that mountain which seems to arise beyond Time into a place which seems also to lie beyond Time, the place '*dove il sol tace*', where the sun is silent, where even Virgil seems but a faint ghost. Virgil is—Virgil, but he is (because of that) poetry, wisdom, institutions, the things that in fact he had been in the world when the great organization of the Empire was formed: all—except the Incarnation. Dante imagines himself here as not able to move on the direct way, as he had in an earlier book imagined Beatrice as dying. He has to go round, through the knowledge of sin and the hellish people 'who have lost the good of intellect'. He has to find another way to the mountain, but when he comes to the ascent he still approaches it under the light of Venus, the dawn star, 'the fair planet which heartens to love'. He has to go through the purging of all sins—especially (he says) of pride. He has to listen to the great discourse of Virgil on the nature of love and the terrible malignancy of the sin which is envy and jealousy and pride. He comes, at the top of the mountain, to the Earthly Paradise of Eden; he sees the procession breaking out of the air, the procession which is the 'Pageant of the Church'. But the final figure of the Pageant of the Church is Beatrice—it is, in fact, a pageant of Beatrice. He sees her; he feels '*d'antico amor . . . la gran potenza*'; he feels the hot embers '*dell' antica fiamma*', and he is answered with what has been called almost the greatest line in Dante and therefore in all poetry:

> *Guardaci ben: ben sem, ben sem, Beatrice.*

Look well: we are, indeed we are, Beatrice.

It is afterwards that he paradisally recovers the perfect knowledge of the good, by drinking of Lethe which removes the knowledge of evil as evil, by drinking of Eunoe which communicates the knowledge of good (even evil) as good. Between the two he sees Beatrice facing the two-natured Gryphon of Christ,

and he sees in her eyes the reflection of those two natures. Those
eyes are not different; they are the very eyes 'from which Love
began to shoot his arrows at you'. Here, surrounded by angels,
prophets, evangelists, virtues, Romantic Love is seen to mirror
the Humanity and Deity of the Redeemer. He sees it; 'my soul
tasted the food which makes hungry where most it satisfies'—so
to combine two poets. It is then that he enters the first heaven
where Piccarda, asked if she does not envy those in greater
heavens their more glorious fate, answers: 'Brother, our will is
quiet in the strength of love . . . here love is fate.' All the ex-
changes of heaven lie open.

But really, though he now imagined it more clearly and more
strongly, he had not known anything different, in essence or in
principle, when the face of the Florentine girl flashed her 'good
morning' at him along the street of their City.

The chance of a phrase joins the theology of Romantic Love to
the theology of the Church. In the *New Life*, at one point,
Beatrice snubs Dante; she 'denies him her salutation'. She had,
he says, heard 'outrageous rumours' about him. After this Love
appeared to him in a vision, and said, '*Ego tamquam centrum
circuli cui simili modo se habent circumferentiae partes; tu autem non
sic*'. Love refused to explain this, but without presuming to do
what Love would not do, one may at least remark that Dante had
experienced humility and goodwill through the salutation. When
the salutation was refused, he was plunged into anything but
humility and goodwill; his beatitude was denied. But Love itself
is not so subjected to outward wants. I do not press that Love
should here be taken as allegorically equal to Christ; I am inclined to think that this develops in the *New Life* but is certainly
not there at the beginning. But Love is certainly sufficiently full
of *caritas* to know that he himself is in the centre and unaffected
by such things on the circumference of experience as salutations
and responses; only with Dante it is not so, or not yet.

About the same time Bonaventura was writing that God was a
circle whose centre was everywhere and its circumference nowhere. The diagram of process is clear. Dante is on the circumference, and the things that happen there make a difference to

him; he has with them no fixed and always equal relation: only he sees the centre. The Love of the *New Life* is in the centre; to it all parts of the circumference, all times, all experiences, have this equal relation. In humility and goodwill Dante answered *Love* when things went well, but Love answers *Love* however things go. But beyond that is the state when there is, in effect, no circumference; or rather, every point of the circumference is at the centre, for the circumference itself is *caritas*, and relation is only between the centre and the centre. This is love-in-heaven.

I have said that I have taken these things—so few of so many —from Dante because they are the expressions of the greatest European poet (greatest as poet, not only as metaphysician) and because no one else has given us so complete an exposition of the Way of Romantic Love. It is, of course, in his own terms; the Way can be followed though the terms are rejected. But at least the Way understood in other terms must not be less than his. It is possible to follow this method of love without introducing the name of God. But it is hardly possible to follow it without proposing and involving as an end a state of *caritas* of the utmost possible height and breadth, nor without allowing to matter a significance and power which (of all the religions and philosophies) only Christianity has affirmed.

If, however, we retain the name and idea of God, and if there is any common agreement about the state of exalted experience known as the state of 'falling in love', then it is possible to go further and relate that experience to the Incarnation of the kingdom. When Messias said: 'Behold my mother' he was, in this relation, merely accurate. The beloved (male or female) is seen in the light of a Paradisal knowledge and experience of good. Christ exists in the soul, in joy, in terror, in a miracle of newness. *Ecce, omnia nova facio.* He who is the mystical child of the lovers sustains and supports them: they are the children of their child. 'We speak that we do know and testify that we have seen. . . . No man hath ascended up into heaven, but he that came down from heaven, even the Son of Man which is in heaven.'

A theology of this kind will be at the disadvantage of all other kinds of theology, and give rise (within itself) to heresies. Extremists of one kind will claim for the beloved a purity as non-existent as the purity of the Church militant upon earth. Her, or his, humanity is an extremely maculate humanity, and all the worship under heaven ought not to prevent her lover from knowing (with reasonable accuracy and unreasonable love) when she is lazy, lewd, or malicious. She has a double nature, and he can have double sight. On the other hand it will be supposed that the death of Beatrice implies the non-existence of Beatrice; that the disappearance of the glory implies the falsity of the glory. A similar disappearance has not been supposed to invalidate the fact and authority of Christ, and the quiet piety—often the extremely quiet piety—of Christians has (justly) been permitted to relate itself to the glory of the Transfiguration. The 'quiet affection' of so many prophecies by the aged might be allowed a similar relation. Quiet piety and quiet affection have their place in the kingdom, but we need not force on them an imperialism they never ought to have at the expense of other more vivid forms of glory and of grace. Nor can the denial or disparagement of those who have forgotten or not experienced it diminish its authority.

It is perhaps a pity that the clergy as a whole are so often among the disparagers. A natural hesitation over the uncovenanted graces leads them not so much to say wrong things as to say the right things in the wrong tone. Their proper concern with one rule of morality leads them to be careless of another. The Divine Thing that made itself the foundation of the Church does not seem, to judge by his comments on the religious leaders of his day, ever to have hoped much from officers of a church. The most he would do was to promise that the gates of hell should not *prevail* against it. It is about all that, looking back on the history of the Church, one can feel they have not done.

Hell has made three principal attacks on the Way of Romantic Love. The dangerous assumptions produced are: (1) the assumption that it will naturally be everlasting; (2) the assumption that it is personal; (3) the assumption that it is sufficient. Similar dangers have attacked other ways in the kingdom; the instance will be remembered of the London churchwarden who had always supposed himself to be a true Christian until one day he realized, in a flash of clarity, that Christ was dogmatically asserted to have died for all men—especially some few whom he strongly disliked and others whom he extremely despised. He therefore, with great good sense, abandoned his profession of Christianity in favour of a free hand with his emotions.

(1) The assumption that the Beatrician state is everlasting is false. 'The right faith is that we believe and confess' that it is eternal but is not everlastingly visible, any more than the earthly life of Christ. Its quality may deceive hasty imagination, and it may be expected to return quickly as was Christ by the Church. It may not. Its authority remains unimpaired. The emotional vows, however, springing from its original state, do not at all times appear so possible or desirable. On the other hand, it seems to be true that there is at first a very strong desire in the two lovers to maintain and conduct for ever this experiment towards *caritas* between themselves, and certainly some kind of pledged fidelity would seem to be a condition of the experiment. The Church has maintained that (under certain conditions) exchanged vows of this kind should be regarded as final. It has even maintained (justly) that, as in certain cases, the state of love leads to marriage, so marriage can lead to a more advanced state of love, and since, on the whole hypothesis, this is the only desirable thing, it may be right in its discipline. (The natural tendency to falsify evidence in favour of a point of view does not perhaps prevail more strongly here than elsewhere.) But the matter of marriage is a subject different from the present and of too lofty a nature to be contented with a paragraph. The appearance of the glory is temporary; the authority of the glory towards pure love is everlasting; the quality of the glory is eternal, such as the heavens have in Christ.

(2) The second assumption is that the state of love is a personal possession; that is, (i) that it is the personal adornment of the beloved; (ii) that it belongs personally to the lover. This mistake is hardly possible in the first state of humility. But the fallen state of man produces—again as in religion—something remarkably like a tendency to regard the revelation and the

glory as one's own private property. Once the emotions have
yielded to that falsity, the intellect too often is either thwarted or
even betrayed into supporting them. Until a state of sanctity has
been achieved, there will no doubt always be something proud or
possessive in our attitude towards the thing that is called love.
But, on the whole hypothesis, love does not belong to lovers, but
they to it. It is their job, as it is their direction, and salvation. It
is for this reason that all such sins as envy and jealousy are mortal. Jealousy does not mean only sex-jealousy; it need not even
relate to the lovers at all. Once the authority of the glory has
been admitted, all jealousy and envy are against the idea of and
the way to *caritas*, but the 'all' must include the sexual. One can
hardly keep jealousy out of the office but let it in to the home. It
is, always and everywhere, idolatry; it is a desire to retain the
glory for oneself, which means that one is not adoring the glory
but only one's own relation to the glory. It ought perhaps, for
fear of misunderstanding, to be added that the strictest mono-
gamist ought to disapprove of jealousy as strongly as anyone
else; the two things are entirely separate. But it must be admitted that we might be a little nearer, intellecually, to pure
love if jealousy had been as passionately denounced as divorce in
the Christian Church. The envious man identifies the kingdom
with himself, and by a frantic effort to retain the outward mani-
festation of the kingdom destroys it in himself, and with it his
capacity to see it outside himself. A sin which is, by its essence,
destructive of goodwill is worse than a sin which need not be, in
its essence, more than disordered goodwill. Virgil proclaimed
the difference; the one kind are bewailed in the place where they
dwell who have lost the good of intellect, the other in the secular
terraces of the Mountain of Purgatory. There is but one permissible state to any who have seen love: '*una fiamma di caritade*', 'a
flame of love'.

(3) The third assumption is even easier than the others: that
it is sufficient to have known that state of love. A kind of Calvin-
ism seizes the emotions; the heart has recognized the attributed
perfection and stops there. It feels as if of the elect, and it goes on
feeling that till it ceases to feel anything. It may recognize a

social duty to be useful to others, to feed the poor. 'Though I give all my goods . . . and have not charity it profiteth me nothing.' To be in love must be followed by the will to *be* love; to be love to the beloved, to be love to all, to be in fact (as the Divine Thing said) perfect.

The alternative is to become the Sir Willoughby Patternes of the spiritual life, and more unbearable even than Meredith's original. Shakespeare gave us the healthy opposite and limit in that as in so much (he, the everlasting corrector of the follies of the disciples of Dante); in our consciousness of such things as regards ourselves we had better not go further than the point at which 'with a pure blush we may come off withal'.

But, independent of any personal error, the vision has remained. It is not limited to love between the sexes, nor to any love. The use of the word (so spoilt has it become) in some sense colours it with the horrid tint of a false adoration and a pseudo-piety. But grace remains grace whatever fruits are grown from it. The experience of communicated humility and goodwill is the experience of the grace of reality and of the kingdom. The kingdom came down from heaven and was incarnate; since then and perhaps (because of it) before then, it is beheld through and in a carnality of joy. The beloved—person or thing—becomes the Mother of Love; Love is born in the soul; it may have its passion there; it may have its resurrection. It has its own divine nature united with our undivine nature. In such a doctrine the Gospels take on other meanings. The light that lighteth every man is seen without as well as within. But that, by definition, is the nature of the kingdom.

CHAPTER VI

The Practice of Substituted Love

Among the epigrams of the kingdom which Saint John arranged in his Gospel immediately before the triumph of the kingdom, he attributed to Messias the saying: 'Greater love hath no man than this that a man lay down his life for his friends.' It is, on a second glance, a doubtful truth. Many men have exhibited their will of love in such a surrender, but many—perhaps more—have exercised among all kinds of hardship a steady tenderness of love besides which the other seems almost easy. But the phrase has to be understood in the content of other meanings. The 'greater love' is distinguished by the 'laying down the life': something similar had been decreed at Sinai: 'thou shalt not see my face, for there shall no man see me and live'. The definition does not, in the Gospels, necessarily mean physical death, even if that is sometimes involved. When Messias said: 'Whosoever will lose his life for my sake and the Gospel's, the same shall find it', he did not confine the promise to the martyrs nor deny to Saint John what he allowed to Saint James. Martyrdom might or might not happen. Saint Paul, in the passage already quoted, denied any value at all to martyrdom unless it were accompanied by *caritas*: 'though I give my body to be burned and have not charity, it profiteth me nothing'. According to the Apostle, self-sacrifice by itself was as remote from the way of salvation as self-indulgence. As a technique, as a discipline, as a method, it might be useful: no more. But so may—if not self-indulgence at least things gratifying to the self. We are not to deny to others the means of their love because those means may seem to indulge us. 'Neither Jew nor Greek, but a new creature.' Neither self-sacrifice, as such, nor self-gratification, as such; both may be sacraments of love at any moment, but neither is covenanted. The denial of the self affects both. 'It is no more I that live, but Christ that liveth in me' is the definition of the pure life which is substituted for both.

The taunt flung at that Christ, at the moment of his most spectacular impotency, was: 'He saved others; himself he cannot save'. It was a definition as precise as any in the works of the medieval schoolmen. It had been already accepted by the action —the action which restrained action—of Messias, as it had been accepted still earlier by his words when he chose necessity. It was an exact definition of the kingdom of heaven in operation, and of the great discovery of substitution which was then made by earth. Earth, at best till then under the control of law, had to find that no law was enough unless the burden of the law, of the law kept or the law unkept, could be known to be borne by heaven in the form of the Holy Thing that came down from heaven. Earth had to find also that the new law of the kingdom made that substitution a principle of universal exchange. The first canon of substitution had been declared in the myth of origin ages before, when the law of man's responsibility for man had been shaped. It had denounced there the first-born child of the Adam, though of the Adam no longer in the union of the knowledge of the good, but in the divided sorrow of conception and of work. The child was Cain, the incarnation of their union outside Paradise, and in some sense of the self-desirous spirit which troubles the divine glory in all lovers. An opposition to goodness was in his nature and is in theirs, a desire to trouble goodness with some knowledge of some kind of evil. He not only killed his brother; he also made an effort to carry on the intellectual falsity which his parents had experienced when they fled from facts in their new shame. He became rhetorical—it is, so early, the first appearance of a false style of words: 'Am I my brother's keeper?' It is a question asked by most people at some moment. 'The voice of thy brother's blood crieth unto me from the ground.' That answer became a law in the covenants: 'At the hand of every man's brother will I require the life of man.'

As the single tyranny of Cain developed into the social tyranny in Egypt and in Israel itself, so the law gathered round itself the clamour of the prophets for social justice: 'seek judgement, relieve the oppressed, judge the fatherless, plead for the widow . . . what mean ye that ye beat my people to pieces, and grind the faces of the poor? saith the Lord God of hosts.' Under the organized effort of Rome towards at least something of the Virgilian equity, this had been defined in the moral duty of all classes and individuals declared by the Precursor; it had become the gospel of the Precursor as of Virgil, except that the one gospel expected beyond itself what the other hardly could. Messias had shown that he would demand and assume its fulfilment by all who wished to follow his own gospel. It had to be left, then, to men to choose or not to choose. The direct concern of the new kingdom was with other things, with the love that had substituted itself for men, and with the love between men that was to form itself after the manner of that original love.

When Messias removed his visibility, he left behind him a group of united followers; he had created the Church. Acts of the Apostles are any guide—say in Chapters ii, iii, iv—the Church began with direct statements of dogma and direct communication of rites. Necessarily, as it spread, it had to organize itself; it had to make decisions on fundamental questions. There was the question, as it grew, of what on certain points it did actually believe; it answered this by finding out in its Councils what in fact it did—in its various localities—actually believe. The message of the Councils to the localities after an inquiry tended to be not so much 'we are telling you what is true' as 'it has been decided that *this* is what the Church actually believes'. Certainly, by rapid development of a hypothesis of its nature, the two things became identical, but there was a difference in method and indeed in idea. Occasionally a Council came to a decision which was not accepted, in which case the hypothesis sooner or later involved the view that it was not a proper Council. For the hypothesis was that there was operative within the Church the sacred and eternal reconciliation of all things, which the Church did not and could not deserve. The Church (it was early decided) was not an organization of sinless men but of sinful, not a union of adepts but of less than neophytes, not of *illuminati* but of those that sat in darkness. Nevertheless, it carried within it an energy not its own, and it knew what it believed about that energy. It was the power of the Reconciler, and the nature of the Reconciler was of eternity as of time, of heaven as of earth, of absolute God as of essential Man. 'Let those who say *There was when he was not* be anathema.'

There was then, so to put it, a new way, the way of return to blissful knowledge of all things. But this was not sufficient; there had to be a new self to go on the new way. This was the difficulty of the Church then as it is now, as it always is after any kind of conversion. There are always three degrees of consciousness, all infinitely divisible: (i) the old self on the old way; (ii) the old self on the new way; (iii) the new self on the new way. The second group is the largest, at all times and in all places. It is the frequent result of romantic love. It forms, at any one moment, the greatest part of the visibility of the Church, and, at most moments, practically all of oneself that one can know, for the new self does not know itself. It consists of the existence of the self, unselfish perhaps, but not yet denied. This self often applies itself unselfishly. It transfers its activities from itself as a centre to its belief as a centre. It uses its angers on behalf of its religion or its morals, and its greed, and its fear, and its pride. It operates on behalf of its notion of God as it originally operated on behalf of itself. It aims honestly at better behaviour, but it does not usually aim at change; and perhaps it was in relation to that passionate and false devotion that Messias asked: 'Think ye when the Son of Man cometh he shall find faith upon the earth?'

Those who accuse the Church accuse it—justly—of not being totally composed of new selves; those who defend it defend it—justly—as being a new way. No doubt the old self on the new way is a necessary period, in most cases, of change. But the Apostles, to judge by the epistles, were not willing that the faithful should remain consistently faithful to themselves. They demanded, as Messias had demanded, that the old self should deny itself. It was to be removed and renovated, to be a branch of the vine, a point of the pattern. It was to become an article of love. And what then is love?

It is possible here to follow only one of the many definitions the New Testament holds; the definition of death. To love is to die and live again; to live from a new root. Part of the experience of romantic love has been precisely that; the experience of being made new, the 'renovation' of nature, as Dante defined it in a particular experience of love. That experience is not sufficient to maintain itself, or at least does not choose to do so. But what is there experienced, and what has been otherwise experienced by many in religion, or outside religion, has to be followed by choice. 'Many are called but few are chosen': we are called from the kingdom but we choose from ourselves. The choice is to affect not only our relation with God but our relation with men. There is to be something of the same kind of relation in it. 'These things have I spoken unto you, that my joy might remain in you, and that your joy might be full.' It is odd how rarely Messias is seen as full of joy—but there it is. He said so; no one else. He proceeded towards our joy: 'This is my commandment, that ye love one another, as I have loved you.' The First Epistle of Saint John carried the same idea, and the Revised Version has it more sharply than the Authorized. 'Hereby know we love, because he laid down his life for us, and we ought also to lay down our lives for the brethren . . . if we love one another, God abideth in us, and his love is perfected in us.' We are to love each other *as* he loved us, laying down our lives *as* he did, that this love may be perfected. We are to love each other, that is, by acts of substitution. We are to be substituted and to bear substitution. All life is to be vicarious—at least, all life in the kingdom of heaven is to be vicarious. The difference between life in the kingdom and life outside the kingdom is to be this. 'Except your righteousness exceed the righteousness of the Scribes and Pharisees, ye shall in no wise enter into the kingdom of Heaven.' But many of the Scribes and Pharisees were good and holy men? yes; what then? it is this love-in-substitution, this vicarious life, which is no more in their law then in the gospel of the Precursor.

The Practice of Substituted Love

'Go, tell John, the blind receive their sight . . . the least in the kingdom of heaven is greater than he.'

It has been the habit of the Church, since the earliest times, ostentatiously to use some such substitution, in one rite at least: in the baptism of infants. It is understood that this is largely due to the persecutions, but also to the nature of the sacrament itself; which was purposed for infants as well as adults, and yet demanded penitence and faith before its operation could be ensured. This responsibility was laid on the godparents: 'at the hand of every man's brother will I require the life of man'. But it is others than infants who can swear more sincerely and more humbly by others' mouths than ever by their own, though it must be with the agreement and desire of their own. It is one of the difficulties of the Church that her presentation of experience does not always coincide with realized experience. The conversion she demands and the sustenance she communicates come sometimes from alien and even from hostile sources; it is one conversion and one sustenance with hers. The invisible Church moves in another manner than the visible; indeed the invisible must include that earthly scepticism, opposition which the visible Church so greatly needs and yet cannot formally include. The sponsors in baptism exhibit the idea of substitution, as that habit which existed in the early Church of being baptized 'for the dead' exhibited it. Part of the fact which such an exhibition ritually and sacramentally presents is the making a committal of oneself from another's heart and by another's intention. It is simpler sometimes and easier, and no less fatal and blessed, to do it so; to surrender and be offered to destiny by another rather than by oneself; it is already a little denial of the self.

But that is as holy Luck may decide. Whatever the means of beginning, the life itself is vicarious. The courtesies of that life are common enough—to lend a book, for example, is a small motion in it, an article of the web of glory. It is the full principle which is defined by the New Testament, and the making of contracts on that principle which exhibit, in the denial of self, the pattern of the web.

87

He came down from Heaven

Saint Paul, in one of those letters which are at once mystical diaries, archiepiscopal charges, and friendly messages, threw out an instruction to the Church at Galatia (Gal. vi, 2). 'Bear ye one another's burdens, and so fulfil the law of Christ.' It is, like the patience of Job, one of our most popular texts. In exterior things it is recognized as valid—at least until we become bored; the fiftieth rather than the first visit to the sick is distasteful. Interiorly, it is less frequently supposed to be possible, and even exteriorly it has a wider range than is, perhaps, allowed. Saint Paul's injunction is to such acts as 'fulfil the law of Christ', that is, to acts of substitution. To take over the grief or the fear or the anxiety of another is precisely that; and precisely that is less practised than praised. 'Mystical substitution' we have heard from the text-books, or from other books that are less than the text-books. It is supposed to be for 'nuns, confessors, saints, not us': so much the worse for us. We are supposed to be content to 'cast our burdens on the Lord'. The Lord indicated that the best way to do so was to hand these over to someone else to cast, or even to cast them on him in someone else. There will still be work enough for the self, carrying the burdens of others, and becoming the point at which those burdens are taken over by the Divine Thing which is the kingdom: 'as he is, even so are we in this world'.

The technique needs practice and intelligence, as much intelligence as is needed for any other business contract. The commerce of love is best established by commercial contracts with man. If we are to make agreements with our adversaries quickly, we ought to be even quicker to make them with our friends. Any such agreement has three points: (i) to know the burden; (ii) to give up the burden; (iii) to take up the burden. It is perhaps in this sense also that Messias said: 'Deny the self, take up the cross, follow me'; it being admitted and asserted that the crucifixion itself is his. He flung out those two seemingly contradictory assertions, he who was rich in contradictions: 'take up the cross', 'my yoke is easy, and my burden is light'. It is not till the cross has been lifted that it can be a burden. It is in the exchange of burdens that they become light. But the carrying of a cross may be light because it is not to the crucifixion. It is 'of faith' that that is done; that is, it is the only part of the work still to be done that we should be fitted into the state where all is done, into the kingdom and the knowledge of everything as good. But a pride and self-respect which will be content to repose upon Messias is often unapt to repose on 'the brethren'. Yet that too is part of the nature of all and of the action of the contract. The one who gives has to remember that he has parted with his burden, that it is being carried by another, that his part is to believe that and be at peace; 'brother, our will is quiet in the strength of love . . . herein love is fate'. The one who takes has to set himself—mind and emotion and sensation—to the burden, to know it, imagine it, receive it—and sometimes not to be taken aback by the swiftness of the divine grace and the lightness of the burden. It is almost easier to believe that Messias was probably right about the mysteries of the Godhead than that he was merely accurate about the facts of everyday life. One expects the burden always to be heavy, and it is sometimes negligible; which is precisely what he said. Discovering that, one can understand more easily the happy abuse he flung at the disciples, say, at the two who went to Emmaus. 'Then he said unto them, O fools and slow of heart to believe all that the prophets have spoken: ought not Christ to have suffered these things and have entered into his glory? And beginning at Moses and all the prophets he expounded unto them in all the scriptures the things concerning himself.'

The giver's part may be harder than the taker's; that is why, here, it may be more blessed to give than to receive, though in the equity of the kingdom there is little difference. It has a greater tendency towards humility and the intellectual denial of the self. In all the high pagan philosophies, now as then, there are many great virtues, and their leaders and teachers often were and are holy and humble men of heart. I do not remember that any of them cried out: 'See how meek and lowly I am!' No Christian has been encouraged to murmur of himself in that state which is called 'the inner chamber' what Christ proclaimed of himself to the world. It is the everlasting difference between the gospel of Christ as one who is to be imitated and one who is to be believed, between one who is an example of living and one who is the life itself; between the philosophies that advise unselfishness as the best satisfaction in life and the religion that asserts exchange to be the only possible means of tolerable life at all. The denial of the self has become metaphysical. He came to turn the world upside-down, and no one's self-respect will stand for that. It is habitual to us therefore to prefer to be miserable rather than to give, and to believe that we can give, our miseries up.

There is, of course, a technique. If A is to carry B's burden he must be willing to do it to the full, even though he may not be asked to do it to the full. It is easy to sentimentalize, but the Day of Judgement exhibits our responsibilities in each case: 'at the hand of every man's brother will I require . . .' Messias may, now, carry the burden if we ourselves deliberately neglect or forget the agreement, but the lucidity of the good knowing the evil as good is likely to exhibit the negligence or forgetfulness as much as the substitution of himself. It is therefore necessary (*a*) not to take burdens too recklessly; (*b*) to consider exactly how far any burden, accepted to the full, is likely to conflict with other duties. There is always a necessity for intelligence.

Our reluctance is inevitably encouraged by the difficulty of carrying out this substitution in the physical world; of developing between men the charismatic ministry. The body is probably the last place where such interchange is possible; it is why Messias deigned to heal the body 'that ye may know that the Son of Man hath power *on earth* to forgive sins'. No such exchange is possible where any grudge—of pride, greed or jealousy —exists, nor any hate; so far all sins must have been 'forgiven' between men. In some states of romantic love it is felt that the power of healing exists, if only it could be brought into action, and on the basis of Romantic Theology it could so be brought into action. We habitually expect too little of ourselves. But it is not only in states of realization that the power exists. It is limited, peculiarly, by other duties. Most men are already so committed that they ought not, whatever their goodwill, to contemplate the carrying of the burden of paralysis or consumption or even lesser things. They are still bound to prefer one good to another. Certainly it is reasonable to believe that the kind of burden might be transmuted into another equivalent kind, and in a full state of the kingdom upon earth such a transmutation would be agreeable and natural. It remains at present an achievement of which our 'faith' is not yet capable. That is no reason why we should not practise faith, a faith in the interchange of the kingdom operating in matter as out of matter, because whatever distinction there may be between the two is only a distinction between modes of love.

It is natural that, in certain happy states (e.g., the Beatrician love), there should be a desire to make any contract of the kind mutual, and so it often may be. At the same time the tendency is sometimes for the pattern not to return but to proceed. The old proverb said that there was always one who kissed and one who took kisses; that too, accepted, is in this sense a part of the pattern. The discovery that one cannot well give back or be given back what one has given or been given in the same place is sometimes as painful as the discovery that one is being loved on principle and not from preference: a good deal of conviction of the equality of all points in the web of the kingdom and of the denial of the self is necessary to make it bearable. Man—fallen man—has, oddly, the strongest objection to being the cause of the practice of *caritas* by someone else. Yet the Apostles in their epistles continually, and necessarily, exhort the faithful to the practice of such a submission: 'let us not love in word, neither in tongue, but in deed and in truth'. To be grateful for what one does not want is a step towards love, even if it is the rather difficult gratitude for the smirk of a well-meaning intercession by the official twice-born in the visible Church. Gratitude is a necessity of all life; it is love looking at the past as faith is love intending the future, and hope is the motion of the shy consciousness of love in the present self; and gratitude, like love, is its own sufficiency:

> *the grateful mind*
> *By owing owes not but still pays, at once*
> *Indebted and discharged.*

He came down from Heaven

It is with the intention of substituted love that all 'inter-cessory' prayer must be charged, and with care that there is no intention of emotional bullying. Even prayer for the conversion of others is apt to be more like prayer for their conversion to the interceder's own point of view than to the kingdom. The old self on the new way has always enjoyed himself most at prayer. He can pray fervently for other people's delivery from other people's sins; he can indicate to Messias where X is wrong; he can try and bring supernatural power to bear on X to stop him or divert him or encourage. It is precisely because he is playing with a real power that this is so dangerous. It is dangerous, for example, to pray that Nero may be delivered from killing Agrippina; it looks a fairly safe petition but . . . What do we know of Nero, of Agrippina, of Messias? But it can never be dangerous, without particularizing, without fluency, intensely to recollect Nero and Agrippina 'in the Lord', nor can it be dangerous to present all pains and distresses to the kingdom with the utmost desire that Messias may be, and the recollection that at that moment he is, the complete reconciliation—through the point that prays, if conditions are so, but if not then through all and any of the points of the kingdom.

'All and any.' We operate, mostly, in sequence, but sequence is not all. 'I am Alpha and Omega, the first and the last, the beginning and the end.' There is no space here to discuss theories of time or the nature of the intercession of the saints. The vicarious life of the kingdom is not necessarily confined to sequence even among the human members of the kingdom. The past and the future are subject to interchange, as the present with both, the dead with the living, the living with the dead. 'The living creatures ran and returned, as the appearance of a flash of lightning.' The laying down of the life is not confined, in the universal nature of the Sole-Begotten, to any points of space or time. It flashes and returns, in a joy, in a distress, and often without joy or distress. Along such threads the glory runs, and along what are, at present, even fainter threads than those. The method of the new life which Messias (he said) came to give so abundantly begins with substitution and proceeds by substitu-

92

tion. No such substitution accents the individual less; on the contrary, it is, for most, the strongest life of the individual. Even in the kingdom of this world those are greatest who (rightly or wrongly) have had assessed to them the desires, wills, lives of others, when Caesar was Rome and Napoleon was France. It is the touch of impersonality in Caesar, the hint that he had in his own strange way denied the self and become only Caesar even to himself that makes him so fascinating. His star burns on the ancient world, as Virgil saw it at Actium, over the homes, the families, the *pietas* of man, before it is answered by the other star that proclaimed the kingdom of a greater substitution.

In the old days David, or whoever wrote the Psalm, exclaimed that no man could redeem or give a ransom for his brother, and in the ultimate sense that is so still, but it was said before the revelation of the secret of evil known as good, and before the mystery of the Atonement of Messias had brought all things into the pattern of the Atonement. All goodness is from that source, changed and exchanged in its process. It was said of the Friars that one went patched for another's rending, and in the kingdom men go glorious for others' labours, and all grown glorious from the labour of all. Messias, after he had spoken to the astonished soul of the five husbands that she had had, and none of them all he—no, not the present lover, however righteous, however holy, he—spoke yet more riddles to the returning Apostles. He looked on the fields, he saw them white to harvest, he cried out of wages and fruit and eternal life, and at once of him that sowed and him that reaped and their common joy. And even as he said it, he flung his words into a wider circuit: 'herein is that saying true, one soweth and another reapeth. I sent you to reap that whereon ye bestowed no labour: other men laboured and ye are entered into their labours.' What! after self-sacrifice and crosses and giving up goods and life, the mind perplexed, the heart broken, the body wrecked—is there not a little success of our own, our own in him, of course, but at least his in us? None; 'I sent you to reap that whereon ye bestowed no labour'. The harvest is of others, as the beginning was in others, and the process was by others. This man's patience shall adorn that man,

and that man's celerity this; and magnificence and thrift exchanged; and chastity and generosity; and tenderness and truth,
and so on through the kingdom. We shall be graced by one and
by all, only never by ourselves; the only thing that can be ours is
the fiery blush of the laughter of humility when the shame of the
Adam has become the shyness of the saints. The first and final
maxim in the present earth is *deny the self*, but—there or here—
when the need for denial has passed, it may be possible to be
astonished at the self as at everything else, when that which is
God is known as the circle whose centre is everywhere and the
circumference nowhere. 'He saved others; himself he cannot
save.' 'The glory which thou gavest me I have given them; that
they may be one, even as we are one: I in them, and thou in me,
that they may be made perfect in one.'

CHAPTER VII

The City

The coming of the kingdom, in myth, in legend, in law, in history, in morals and metaphysics, has been the coming of a thing at once exclusive of all things and inclusive of everything. All the threads of the pattern have that nature, and the whole pattern is of the same nature.

All the gospels are full of that inclusive-exclusive command to do things 'for my sake'. It is the definition of *caritas*, and *caritas* is the nature of the kingdom. It is habitually set against *eros*, the personal love, and distinguished as being a kind of impersonal goodwill. If goodwill is taken to mean the *voluntas inflammata*, the fiery wheel of the prophets, it will serve; unfortunately, nothing is less like a fiery wheel than the hobnailed boots of ordinary moral effort. They are hardly nailed with joy. The Passion of Messias, for all its grief, was accompanied by discourses of delight and joy—at least in the arrangement of the Gospels.

'It is man's duty', said Johnson, 'to be happy.' It is not enough to be full of an effort towards goodwill unless it is a joyous goodwill. 'The Spirit of glory is upon you', said Saint Peter, contemplating persecutions and martyrdoms. The very idea—the very distant idea—of more pain and distress than ordinary life supplies is enough to chill the blood in our already pallid happiness. It was the consciousness of the extreme surrender and the sadness which must accompany it that caused one Christian poet to compose a hymn with the refrain:

> *Jesus Christ is our Redeemer*
> *And we wish to God he weren't*

He came down from Heaven

His intelligence was lamentable but his emotion was comprehensible. We are unhappy enough anyhow, and if Christianity is to mean a little more unhappiness, more discipline, more trials—the prospect not unnaturally drives men to that plea for annihilation which (the Church declares) is the only thing the Omnipotence will never grant, except indeed by the annihilation which is he. On the other hand, there is an offensive cheerfulness encouraged by some Christians which is very trying to any person of moderate sensibility. We are to be bright; we are to smile at strangers; we are (last horror of daily life!) to get into conversation with strangers. It is some comfort to reflect that Messias was against our being bright as he was against our being gloomy. He was against our being anything at all. He indicated continually that it was our wish to do or be something by ourselves, even to be saved by ourselves, that was the root of the trouble. It is at least possible for some of us easily to deny ourselves any tendency towards a communal cheerfulness.

The word that runs through the Bible, the word that defines the yonder side of the demanded *caritas*, is glory. It is glory which in the Old Testament from a general brightness becomes a mathematical splendour; it is glory which accompanies, in the New, the first beginning of signs when water is suddenly poured out as wine; it is communicated to the disciples—'the glory which thou gavest me I have given them'; it accompanies the City that slides from the utmost heavens into the sight of Patmos. In the Gospel of Saint John the word is particularly associated with action; it is the acts of Messias which form the glory. The first miracle is his glory. He says to Martha just before the raising of Lazarus (in answer to her: 'Lord, by this time he stinketh'): 'Said I not unto thee, that, if thou wouldest believe, thou shouldst see the glory of God?' He promises the Apostles: 'whatsoever ye shall ask in my name, that will I do, that the Father may be glorified in the Son'. He looks forward to the Passion: 'The hour is come that the Son of Man should be glorified . . . Father, save me from this hour: but for this cause came I unto this hour. Father, glorify thy name.' The last discourse is a torrent of glory; the last prayer a declaration of com-

municated glory, that is, of communicated acts. The pattern of
the glory is a pattern of acts.

The fulfilment of all things has been, traditionally, described
twice in the Bible: once in the Song of Solomon, once in the
Apocalypse. The first, as has been often pointed out (significantly
by Sue in *Jude the Obscure*), is a love-poem or a set of love-poems,
or a drama of love (critical opinion is variable); the second is a
revolutionary pamphlet. The *Encyclopaedia Britannica* says of
the first, and might have said of the second, that 'its oriental
standard of taste differs from that of the modern West'. In spite
of that, neither book has been without its effect on the modern
West, and even on the taste of the modern West. The doves and
harts of the one and the sea monster of the other have lingered in
our literature and in our thought. More particularly, the 'community' has lingered, for in both the mystical tradition has
thought of the universal and not of the individual. The chapter-
headings of the first refer the passion and the joy not to Christ
and the soul but to Christ and the Church; and the very text of
the other contains the vision not of the soul apostate or redeemed
but of the City. The idea of the kingdom has always had some
content of revolution and of love, however conventional and
prosaic the visible Church has made them; for the maxim of the
kingdom is that of all love and all revolution: *ecce, omnia nova
facio*—behold, I make all things new.

'And I saw a new heaven and a new earth . . . and I John saw
the holy city . . . descending out of heaven from God, having the
glory of God: and her light was like unto a stone most precious,
even like a jasper stone, clear as crystal.' It is like the 'terrible
crystal' which was over the heads of the living creatures in
Ezekiel; and perhaps it is not entirely irrelevant to think of that
crystal as being over the heads of all those great other monsters
which loom in vast significances through all such art—the horse
of Job among the trumpets, and the Leviathan that is no play-
mate for girls, and the camel that is too huge for a needle's eye
however enlarged, and the eagles on which in the time of
Exodus Israel was to be brought to the Lord. The new earth and
the new heaven come like the two modes of knowledge, know-

ledge being the chief art of love, as love is the chief art of knowledge: earth a directness, heaven a substitution. The City—hold-
ing both—is the formulation of that old prophecy—'a kingdom
of priests . . . they shall teach no more every man his neighbour,
and every man his brother, saying: Know the Lord; for they
shall all know me, from the least of them unto the greatest of
them, saith the Lord.' The same thing is said of the City: 'I saw
no temple therein . . . the Lord God Almighty and the Lamb are
the temple of it . . . the Lord God giveth them light.' The centre
is everywhere and the circumference nowhere; that is, it is
hierarchic and republican at once, as all good states, even on this
present earth, are known to be, where everything and everyone
is unique and is the subject of due adoration so, and yet, all
being unique, 'none is afore or after other, none is greater or less
than another'.

Those who are excluded from the City are 'whoever loveth
and maketh a lie'. This too is the intellectual falsity of the beginning, the 'making of aprons' of the myth and the prophets pro-
phesying falsely of Jeremiah; it is, obviously, excluded from the
City because, anyhow, it cannot see the City, or if, not as a place
to be entered. 'The people who have lost the good of intellect'
cannot exist at the highest point of intellect, the point where all
is brought out into clarity, 'with every secret thing'. It is this
which has distinguished the doctrines of Christendom; nothing
is to be lost or forgotten; all things are to be known. They can
be known as good, however evil, for they can be known as occasions of love. But known they must and shall be: 'the Lord God
giveth them light'. Messias and the New Testament know
nothing about blotting out the past. Messias insists on making it
prominent. It is natural to a doctrine which has not hesitated to
make its God responsible for all; responsible in this sense—that
knowing with a clarity inconceivable to man everything that
would happen in his creation he yet ordained the creation. No
amount of pious exposition of the freewill of man can avoid that
fact. There is no split second of the unutterable horror and
misery of the world that he did not foresee (to use the useless-
ness of that language) when he created; no torment of children,

no obstinacy of social wickedness, no starvation of the innocent,
no prolonged and deliberate cruelty, which he did not know. It is
impossible for the mind of man to contemplate an infinitesimal
fraction of the persistent cruelty of mankind, and beyond mankind of the animals, through innumerable years, and yet remain
sane. 'The whole creation groaneth and travaileth together in
pain.' The Omnipotence contemplated that pain and created;
that is, he brought its possibility—and its actuality—into existence. Without him it could not have been; and calling it his permission instead of his will may be intellectually accurate, but
does not seem to get over the fact that if the First Cause has
power, intelligence, and will to cause a universe to exist, then he
is the First Cause of it. The First Cause cannot escape being the
First Cause. All the metaphors about fathers giving their children opportunities to be themselves fail, as all metaphors fail.
Fathers are not the First Cause. God only is God. The pious
have been—as they always are—too anxious to excuse him; the
prophet was wiser: 'I form the light and create darkness: I make
peace and create evil: I the Lord do all these things.'

But other religions have gone so far; Christianity has gone
further. It has proclaimed that the Omnipotence recognized that
responsibility in the beginning and from the beginning, and
acted on it—not by infusing grace only but by himself becoming
what himself had made, in the condition to which it had, by his
consent, brought itself. It is this particular act, done of free choice
and from love, which makes the Faith unique. All the deities, and
all the sacrificed deities, the sun-myths and the vegetable simu-
lacra, all that look much like the God of Christianity, look in the
last analysis much unlike the God of Christianity. There is over
all of them a Fate, or else there is no union with man. But
Christian dogma has denied all Fate behind the Omnipotence as
Alfred denied it in his translation of Boethius a thousand years
ago. 'But I say, as do all Christian men, that it is the divine purpose that rules them, not Fate.' It has asserted the indivisible
union of the two natures in the single Person. It has asserted that
this union accepted responsibility; at the hand of God himself
God has required the life of man.

He came down from Heaven

It is from this fact that the City descends to Patmos and the world. The descent of the City, in its web of exchanged glory, is the definition of the necessary *caritas*, the 'for my sake' of the gospels. The stress of love in man has altered. There is only one reason why anything should be loved on this earth—because God loves it. Beatrice (whoever and whatever Beatrice may be) is no longer to be loved for the gratification of the lover, in however pure or passionate a sense. She is no longer to be loved for herself alone; that is perhaps the height of ordinary inventions of literature, and it was much as is generally suggested. Beatrice anyhow is generally, and naturally, satisfied with that. But the kingdom of heaven is not satisfied. Beatrice is to be loved 'for my sake'. It sounds simple, and is difficult. It is the change in the laying down of the love and the life, hinted at by those masters of the spiritual way who speak of the soul abandoning the love of created things before she can find God. It is precisely *her* love— her own love of created things—that she abandons, and her own consciousness of love; and she may then, not improperly, when they say to her, 'thy mother and thy brethren', look at all things round her and answer, 'Behold my mother and my brethren'. The law of exchange is the mother of the soul; and this too is that other curious promise of Messias, when he committed himself to the statement that those who had given up anything for his sake should have its equivalent multitudinously restored—as in the book of Job. 'Verily I say unto you, There is no man that hath left house, or parents, or brethren, or wife, or children, for the kingdom of God's sake, who shall not receive manifold more in this present time, and in the world to come life everlasting.' It has not been generally observed that things seem to happen so, perhaps because there is a heavenly catch in the promise, after all. Messias is certainly to be trusted, but only after his own manner. 'He is his own interpreter', as a once popular hymn justly remarks. He is; no one else could begin to think of his interpretations. 'My thoughts are not your thoughts.' One cannot object; that is the nature of God, but it makes things more difficult. Saint Paul defined the restoration in another epigram: 'having nothing, yet possessing all things'. It is the custom of the City.

The City

As the acts of Messias are historic and contemporary at once, so the coming of the City is contemporary and future at once. It is to be (the Church has affirmed), but also it is now. There are, now, flashes and hints of a state in which preference has disappeared. Things are merely good, and their only elements are peace and joy. There is no law to control these moments and no guide to direct us to them. They only exist. They have that additional grace that they redeem us from a too specialized imprisonment in a terminology. It is necessary to have words for things, and it is helpful to recognize things by words. It is also possible to come under the tyranny of special forms of words. The thing we call 'grace' is here and there and gone and back, like the lightning of the living creatures, and a greater: 'so shall also the coming of the Son of Man be'. It is a kind of life, and in that life we are for a moment no more ourselves. It is a life admirably described in the Apocalypse as drinking freely of the waters of life in the City, so simple, so natural, so one with all. It is to that life that the two images in the Bible of the Consummation addressed themselves, each at the end of its utterance. The Shulamite ends: 'make haste, my beloved, and be thou like to a roe or to a young hart upon the mountains of spices'. The witness in the Apocalypse ends: 'He which testifieth these things saith: Surely I come quickly. Amen. Even so, come, Lord Jesus.'

The organic word of prayer which Messias conveyed to his disciples unites the City with its reflections upon earth. The descent from heaven reaches that prayer, utters it, stays in it, and turns again in it towards the re-ascent. The living creatures of heaven run up and down on it, desiring, with that blaze of intellectual curiosity characteristic of heaven, to understand the relations in which they share; and on it also all sharers of exchange on earth. The prayer opens with an invocation of beatitude in its provident relation towards us. It proclaims and invokes the sanctity of that heaven in all its types upon earth. The name of God is that which all creation, in its different kinds and degrees, aspires to know, to utter, and to become. Its life is in that; all difference is in the mode of knowledge. It invokes the kingdom, following on the prophecy of the Precursor and the

royal incantation of Messias—let it emerge; let the name become the kingdom and the flashing and glorious moments of love
be a pattern and an order and an instinct and no less themselves.
It entreats for earth the pure and absolute knowledge of earth in
the same manner in which that knowledge already exists in the
heaven of the eternal beatitude; let us understand the completion
even here, the completion of all and of this very event in which
we are now engaged, the peace of the determination of the Will
as it is already fulfilled. It desires, for that end, the nourishment
of all beings, but especially of men, in all states—the bread
which is the joy. It touches, then, on a thing which, known to us
too bitterly here, is (one way or another) still known in heaven
—the ardent interchange of pardon; but now is its grand terror,
in a word as short as any in the prayer, in the little monosyllable
'as'. 'Forgive us . . . *as* we forgive . . .' in the manner that . . . to
the extent that . . . This is the acceptance of the government of
Messias, the assent to the law of interchange, the accommoda-
tion of heaven to our intention upon earth. It is at once our
humility towards and our control upon heaven; the casting off or
the drawing-down of rule and measurement by ourselves and for
ourselves. Forgive us *as*—and then the thing, as if startled at its
own daring and shocked at its own danger, rushes up into a
heavenly fear: 'lead us not into temptation', do not abandon us
to such a trial: what is the nothingness that is we to do there?
deliver us, deliver us from evil, from the evil that man chose
once to know, the evil of split knowledge and the agony of the
good turned against itself, the evil therefore of the deprivation of
good, of the loss of joy, the illusion of love in the self and the
monstrous duplicities that follow the self: deliver us, deliver us.
'Thou only art holy, thou only art the Lord'; 'without thee
Nothing is strong——' out of that Nothing deliver us, by ourselves becoming nothing to ourselves, having no power to be
except in the kingdom. 'For thine is the kingdom'—the three
changes of the great transmutation follow; 'thine is the kingdom, and the power, and the glory', the web, and the operation
down all the threads of the web, and the eternal splendour of
threads and web at once. 'This also is Thou'—not that we can

102

ever know the glory in itself; at the height of all knowledge, all knowledge drops—'neither is this Thou'.

To think of the pattern is not to be part of the pattern; to talk of exchange is not to exchange. The division between the old self and the new is greater than any distinction between the ways, though the ways are important. Saint Paul feared the danger that Messias implied: 'they who say Lord, Lord, and do not the things that I say'; 'lest when I have preached to others, I myself should be a castaway'. Christendom has demanded the closest examination of conscience to avoid that retrogression, but our motions slide down, one below the other, and the schism of intention is deeper than any other; where is certainty? who can be sure of any motive in any act? Yet the choice, the wish that may become the will, may be there, whatever our ignorance; to desire to follow the good is important, to desire to follow the good from the good is more important. Saint John eased the young Church: 'if our hearts condemn us, God is greater than our hearts, and knoweth all things'. Messias himself condescended to encouragement in the parable of the tares. 'Sow good seed; but when good and evil spring up together, and all a mixed growth in the heart, do not fret, do not go hunting among motives for blades of wheat here and blades of tares there. I will separate all, I will save these and annihilate those; be at peace, be glad, leave decision to me. Only sow; work while it is yet day.' In all communicated joy there is the sense of three great sayings. The first is the joyous mockery of Messias: 'O fools and slow of heart to believe . . .' The second is his definition: 'I am Alpha and Omega, the beginning and the end, the first and the last.' The third is the threat which must inevitably accompany the coming of the heavenly thing on to earth: 'Blessed is he whosoever shall not be offended at me.'

THE FORGIVENESS OF SINS

To
THE INKLINGS

CHAPTER I

Introduction

How is it possible to write a book on the Forgiveness of Sins? It is impossible. Great poets might do it, for they understand everything; and saints, for they are united with everything—creatures as well as Creator.

'I did pray all creatures', wrote Angela of Foligno, '(seeing how that I had offended them inasmuch as I had offended the Creator), that they would not accuse me before God. Then did it appear unto me that all creatures and all the saints did have compassion upon me, wherefore with a greater fire of love did I apply myself to praying unto God more than was customary.'

The principles of the universe are clear to both those groups of sufferers. But other writers, who only repeat, more or less intelligently, with more or less goodwill, what they have been told; popularizers of the spirit whose duty is to the next moment; pedants and propagandists and other plagiarists of man's heart—what do we know about it? what can we say with any conviction, and with any style, of the crises of the spirit? We follow the fashion; the fashion, in our set, is to talk religion precisely as in other sets they talk films or finance. So we talk or we write; and, not having a high style to write in, not being able to manage words, we naturally persuade ourselves that colloquialisms and clichés are desirable. We must write for Everyman, and because it is reported that Everyman is crude, we must write crudely for him.

Yet if there is one thing which is obviously either a part of the universe or not—and on knowing whether it is or not our life depends—it is the forgiveness of sins. Our life depends on it in every sense. If there is God, if there is sin, if there is forgiveness, we must know it in order to live to him. If there are men, and if forgiveness is part of the interchanged life of men, then we must know it in order to live to and among them. Forgiveness, if it is at all a principle of that interchanged life, is certainly the deepest of all; if it is not, then the whole principle of interchange is false. If the principle of retributive justice is our only hope we had certainly better know it. Because then, since retributive justice strictly existing everywhere is staringly impossible, all our hopes of interchange and union, of all kinds, are ended at once; and we had better know *that*.

It is not, however, in this human discussion of the possibilities of forgiveness that the dark terror lies. We can happily universalize our individual experiences into theories there without feeling much horror, though not perhaps without doing some harm. The fear is in making statements about God. There both the possibility of truth and the possibility of communication fail. Neither rhetoric nor meiosis will serve; the kingdom of heaven will not be defined by inexact terms, and exact terms. . . . Exact terms! It is not altogether surprising that we are driven back sometimes on irony, even on a certain bitterness. At least, so, we acknowledge the impossibility of the task; besides, we may find that our ironies are merely true. Irony is perhaps cheap but it is useful: it is (to use a metaphor itself ironic, cheap, and useful) a gas-mask against heaven. It is true we shall find we are carefully wearing it against pure air—that is the irony. But we should not at first have been able to bear the pure air without protection—that is the truth. It was the laughter of Beatrice in heaven which had once to be spared Dante—her laughter and heaven's song. The false smile of irony spares us for a while from the true smile of heaven.

All then that can really be hoped is that some semi-attentive reader, distrusting or despising what he reads, may turn from it to consider in himself the nature of forgiveness; so, and only so, can this consideration hope to be of any use. It is, as our Lord told us long ago, only the compulsion of the soul that leads to a true knowledge of the doctrine. It is true the comprehension of the blood beats with the same knowledge, though there not understood. Discussion and speculation are amusing enough; there are twenty-four hours in every day and they have to be got through somehow. Any fool can invent theories of the Fall, and when fools were interested in theology they frequently did; nowadays they are more concerned with economics or strategy or 'ideals'. Any fool can discuss how or what God, from his pure self-existence, knows, creates, or sustains. Even in reading the great doctors we sometimes become conscious of a sudden revolt, not perhaps in itself unwise. 'The holy intellect', 'our blessed reason'—we are like Wordsworth; we are bound to

> *deem our blessed reason of least use*
> *Where wanted most.*

The application of the finite to the infinite must surely always be wrong? Since we can never have all the premises, how can our conclusions ever be true? Just; yet the blood holds the need; our physical natures awake thought and even in some sense think; they measure good and evil after their kind. The easy talk of mental distress being worse than physical may occasionally be true; only occasionally. Most men would prefer a month's mental distress to a month's serious neuralgia. It is in our bodies that the secrets exist. Propitiation, expiation, forgiveness, are maintained *there* when the mind has explained them away—the need, and the means, and the fruition.

The secrets of extreme heaven and the secrets of extreme earth are both obscure to us. It is between these realities that explanation and diagram inadequately lie. The ways of approach are two. One may begin by considering pardon as a fact in human life, and so proceed to a meditation on its nature as a divine act. Or one may begin by considering it as a divine act and so conclude with the human. Discussions of human experience are nearly always unsatisfactory. To ask 'do we not all know?' or 'have we not all felt?' by the mere phrasing of the sentence convinces the reader that he has neither known nor felt. But some idea of pardon as men have known it is necessary as a description if not as a definition. The only safe place to find it is in those writers who have been able to put it in undeniable phrases—especially in the poets. I propose therefore first to examine how forgiveness is presented in Shakespeare; afterwards how it appears in the theology of the Christian Church; and finally, how it operates, or should operate, among men.

CHAPTER II

Forgiveness in Shakespeare

Forgiveness in Shakespeare is of three kinds, (i) the merely formal, (ii) the developed situation, as in *Measure for Measure*, (iii) the spontaneous reality in the last plays. Over (i) no time need be spent. As good an example as any is in the early *Two Gentlemen of Verona*. The play has to end, and the innocent hero and his outlaw associates have to be restored. The associates therefore are said to be 'reformed', and the Duke generally forgives them all. But we cannot take it at all seriously; they are forgiven, as they were outlawed, for the convenience of the play, and for all the interest we have in them they might as well have been executed at once. No one would have cared. Much the same is true of the other earlier comedies; whenever it is needed, there is always a reach-me-down forgiveness at hand. Shakespeare was not yet interested in what happens when men forgive. The most that can be said is that faults are overlooked: 'all right, we won't say any more about it' is the general attitude.

(ii) A much more moving scene occurs during the last act of *Measure for Measure*. This is supposed to belong to the middle period of Shakespeare's career, after the early comedies and the histories and before the great tragedies. At this time Shakespeare was showing signs of going all 'intellectual'. He wrote several plays which might almost be called problem-plays—that is, they involved some kind of moral or philosophical question, though this was, of course, as was always Shakespeare's way, subordinated to the expression of the human heart. He did, in fact, abandon the intellectual method; or perhaps it would be truer to say that he absorbed it into the other more inclusive

111

method. *Troilus and Cressida*, which was written about this time, has a definite philosophical discussion of the nature of value; it is the only thing of its kind in Shakespeare. *Measure for Measure* has nothing of that sort, but even *Measure for Measure* has a less normal plot than is customary with Shakespeare; it is indeed almost abnormal. It is the problem of a man naturally chaste, almost (could the phrase be allowed) naturally holy, though a little over-austere, tempted to lust and murder by the sight of a woman who is to him precisely a vision of chastity and sanctity. The situation is not, certainly, as abnormal as all that; in our experiences sensuality and sanctity are so closely intertwined that our motives in some cases can hardly be separated until the tares are gathered out of the wheat by heavenly wit. The tale of the play is known well enough. Angelo is chaste, and being made governor of Verona instead of the Duke who pretends to go on a journey, condemns a young man named Claudio to death (according to the law) for having intercourse with a girl, before marriage. Isabella, Claudio's sister, a novice of Saint Clare, appeals to the Deputy for her brother's pardon. He falls in love with her, and offers her the pardon in exchange for her consent to his lust.

> *O cunning enemy, that to catch a saint*
> *With saints dost bait thy hook*[1]

There is no need to digress into further coils. By a trick his earlier pledged love Mariana is substituted for Isabella. But when the night is ended Angelo orders Claudio to be executed. The Duke returns and all the evil is brought to light.

It is now that the scene of pardon opens. It is not perhaps composed, except here and there, of great poetry; but we are not here concerned with it as poetry, but with the diagram that is expressed in the poetry. Angelo himself, when all is discovered, begs for punishment.

> *Then, good prince,*
> *No longer session hold upon my shame,*
> *But let my trial be my own confession.*
> *Immediate sentence then and sequent death*
> *Is all the grace I beg.*

The Duke condemns him. But Mariana pleads for his pardon, and in her anguish begs Isabella to plead with her. The Duke protests that such a request is 'against all sense'. Mariana continues to invoke Isabella: and at the very last moment Isabella, realizing fully that Angelo has meant to seduce her and kill her brother (and supposing he has certainly done the last), suddenly yields. She kneels before the Duke; in a grave and very moving line, she begins:

> *Most bounteous sir,*
> *Look, if it please you, on this man condemned.* . . .

She intercedes; she says all that can be said on his behalf; she asks for his pardon. The play moves on to its end, but that moment has been seized by the way.

What is of interest here is that, by chance or by choice, Shakespeare allows the two persons between whom the wrong existed to make to the Duke two opposed requests. He who has caused the wrong asks for his punishment; she who has suffered it asks for his pardon. I am always reluctant to draw from the plays any deductions, except in the most general terms, about Shakespeare's personal opinions; and I do not suggest that we have any right to be shocked, after this scene, when we find Shakespeare claiming payment of debts due to him in the law-courts. Nor, on the other hand, ought we to neglect this poetic moment because of Shakespeare's personal behaviour. It may be but an accident of the conclusion of the play. But it is an intense and exciting accident, and its excitement and intensity depend on the greatness of the wrong done to Isabella, on her pause before she consents to ask the Duke to forgive, and on the reciprocal attitude of the two concerned. We recognize the power of the idea.

(iii) In the tragedies the question of forgiveness does not arise. It may be said that that is one reason why they are tragedies. The hesitation to regard oneself as wronged, the capacity not to brood over wrong—this itself is lacking in Hamlet and Othello. It is a personal grudge, indulged, which distracts both of them. The wrongs of Lear are lost in madness; the sins of Macbeth are offered no chance of pardon. That is the nature of those plays.

The Forgiveness of Sins

But in the last comedies something else enters at the end—pardon certainly, but no longer the serious and considered pardon of *Measure for Measure*. Now pardon has no longer to compel itself to move; it moves at once; it runs. It is again to be allowed that this is the solution which the different style of those last plays demanded. But at least the imagination of Shakespeare was able to discover such a solution. In *Measure for Measure* pardon had been a delayed and virtuous determination of Isabella's chaste and devoted mind. But in *Cymbeline* it is so swift that it seems almost to create the love to which it responds. The noblest of Shakespeare's women, Imogen, has been condemned by her husband Posthumus to death for (as he thinks) disloyalty. She supposes him to be in love with someone else, and to desire her death, and she rebukes him to herself with the phrase:

> *My dear lord,*
> *Thou art one of the false ones.*

It is the tenderest reproach in literature. But in the last act she does not wait for him to ask her forgiveness; the word is not named. It is true that he has in fact already repented of his intention to have her killed, though he still believes her guilty. But the supposed murder lies heavy on him and, solitary and in prison, he broods upon it. He also desires to die on her account, though he does not think the gods, 'more clement than vile men', desire it. His repentance is by them 'desired more than constrained'. The gods made his life, and therefore (and only therefore) it may be weighed equal with Imogen's. He has a passion for repentance, and perhaps it is this yielding of his life which is, to himself, the only exposition of repentance. He is so far worthy of and prepared for her forgiveness. But the real difference is in the resentment and the lack of resentment with which they separately feel the original offence, real or supposed.

In the final crisis she turns to him with a cry of protest-in-love and of renewal-in-love:

> *Why did you throw your wedded lady from you?*
> *Think that you are upon a rock, and now*
> *Throw me again.*

114

Forgiveness in Shakespeare

She can even make a play upon the word 'throw' in her high delight; and Posthumus can only accept the beauty with a renewed fidelity. It is true that they are in a special relationship of love; the other pardons in the play are of a more distant kind and have to be more formally expressed. The last act of *Cymbeline*, let it be admitted, is a wild dance of melodramatic recognitions and long-lost children with strawberry-marks. But the style of Imogen is the keynote of all; the pardon of Imogen the pattern of all; and both style and pardon, though so heavenly, are as realistic as anything in Shakespeare. Her father says of her that she looks at those present, hitting

> *each object with a joy; the counterchange*
> *Is severally in all.*

As if in that 'counterchange of joy' Posthumus says to his enemy —but this time after an expressed grief:

> *Kneel not to me.*
> *The power that I have on you is to spare you,*
> *The malice, to forgive.*

And the king follows with:

> *Pardon's the word to all.*

The thought is even carried on into the final—and political— settlement. The king has conquered the Romans, but he then proposes to submit and pay the tribute, the refusal of which had been the occasion of the war. There is, in this sense, a peculiar fitness in the departure of the persons of the play to the temple of Jupiter:

> *Let's smoke the temple with our sacrifices.*

Such a departure is, certainly, a dramatic expedient for getting them off the stage, and it is not accompanied by any great lines of verse; it need not therefore be taken too carefully. Still, for what it is worth, it is there; and it is worth precisely *that* choice of departure instead of any other—feasts or weddings or what not.

115

The Forgiveness of Sins

The theme of pardon is therefore more expressed in *Cymbeline* than in the other two late comedies. It may be repeated that no deduction can be made from the plays concerning Shakespeare's personal life. He may or he may not have wished, or indeed been able, to forgive those (if any) who had injured him as he imagined Imogen forgiving. But at least he understood such a forgiveness; and took a poetic advantage of it. The carelessness of style he pretended to show in those last plays—as if the most wonderful phrases fell from him by chance—is the full maturity of style: *ars celare artem*—it was his lordliest art to pretend that his art was nothing. And this too is, artistically, the cause of his phrasing of the speed of pardon; he would not have it heavy. But the realistic style reflects a realism: this is what the loveliest pardon is—it is love renewing itself in a mutual and exchanged knowledge.

In the other two late comedies the nature of pardon is not so definitely expressed: its speed and reality is left to the fact that nothing is said, or hardly anything. In the *Winter's Tale* the only phrase is

> *Both your pardons*
> *That ere I put between your holy looks*
> *My ill suspicion.*

The reconciliations accept this and seem courteously to set it aside, but they do not verbally comment on it. The comment they imply is given in Prospero's speech in the *Tempest*. There one of the wrongdoers exclaims:

> *O how odd 'twill sound that I*
> *Must ask my child forgiveness ;*

and Prospero answers:

> *There, sir, stop.*
> *Let us not burden our remembrance with*
> *A heaviness that's gone.*

This answer comes somewhere between Isabella's deliberateness and Imogen's speed: it has a grave joy of its own, but that joy

116

Forgiveness in Shakespeare

consists in forgetting rather than in recollecting the past. These two methods are the double technique of pardon; we shall have occasion to consider them both presently.

It has seemed worth while recalling these Shakespearian moments for several reasons. They are the infinite statement of a certain human experience without reference to anything but itself. They are the finest expressions of that experience in English verse. And they include various types, or (say) methods of pardon. There is the deliberate—and (in the play) it is to be supposed religious—act of Isabella; pardon corresponding to penitence, and penitence demanding penalty as pardon offers freedom: a union of passions, but a grave and deliberate union. Such was the power of Shakespeare's middle style: he reached the deep human experiences by a noble sound of approach; there is a kind of ceremony in the verse—'Most bounteous sir . . .' But after that, and after the tragedies, he reached a new kind of style, and took full advantage of it. Love was never so much mere love; death never so much mere death; jealousy never so much mere jealousy; pardon never so much mere pardon as there.

I do not deny that this high realization of pardon may have derived from the Christian religion. But we must not say that Shakespeare showed it as so deriving. It is clear that he gave it to personages in whom he implied no touch of what the theologians call grace. I am aware that he used the word a number of times, and off and on. But no one has yet, I think, tried to prove that Imogen was a devout Christian woman. It is her glory that she is purely natural; it is her double glory that her nature holds within it a state of being equivalent, one might say, to sanctity. Further than that glorious youth—beautiful, frank, fierce, and direct—Shakespeare had no opportunity to pursue her, for the play had an end, and Imogen. But if a fancy might be permitted, it would be that the old age of Imogen was as wise as her youth, and her power of lucid pardon never slothful; that 'all her acts', in the phrase with which Florizel in the *Winter's Tale* praised Perdita—'all her acts were queens'. It is towards that state of being that forgiveness aims; the sufficiency of the actions of the soul need this virtue as their condition.

117

The Forgiveness of Sins

There are, of course, other poets in whom the theme of forgiveness appears; not, perhaps, so many. It is not, I think, actually in Shelley, for all his lyric song about the disappearance of evil; at least, the difficulty of it is not there. It is in Milton, as it is in Dante, but in both it is, or is meant to be, a Christian pardon, and it will be more convenient to discuss that directly in its own nature rather than indirectly in them. It is certainly in Blake, and he may enter presently as a comment on the theme; it is in Browning's *Ring and the Book,* and in that poem Pompilia again casts the word aside—

> *I—pardon him? . . .*
> *I am saved through him,*
> *So as by fire; to him, thanks and farewell.*

It is not, I think, much in later poets, who are concerned more with the agony than the solution, with ironic or tragic themes rather than with those of comedy. But forgiveness is the resolution of all into a kind of comedy, the happiness of reconciliation, the peace of love.

CHAPTER III

The Sin of Adam

This then is the Shakespearian statement of pardon, and it is put forward here as a high presentation of human experience. It is not especially religious in spite of the semi-religious setting, though it is certainly capable of a profound religious interpretation. But it does not, to all readers, necessarily involve that; it can be, for atheists as well as Christians, a maxim of the normal human intelligence. This, one way or another, whatever else it may be, whatever the cause may be, is what forgiveness between men must be. It remains to consider it in relation to the particular Christian pattern of the universe.

The beginning of all this specific creation was the Will of God to incarnate.[1] God himself is pure spirit; that is, in so far as any defining human word can apply to him, he is pure spirit. He had created matter, and he had determined to unite himself with matter. The means of that union was the Incarnation; that is, it was determined that the Word was to be flesh and to be man.

It is clear that this, like all his other acts, might have been done to himself alone. It was certainly not necessary for him to create man in order that he might himself become man. The Incarnation did not involve the Creation. But it was within his Nature to will to create joy, and he willed to create joy in this manner also.

He willed therefore that his union with matter in flesh should be by a mode which precisely involved creatures to experience

---

[1] It will be obvious from what follows that I am here following one arrangement of doctrine rather than what is perhaps the more usual. But I am instructed that it is no less orthodox.

joy. He determined to be incarnate by being born; that is, he determined to have a mother. His mother was to have companions of her own kind; and the mother and her companions were to exist in an order of their own degree, in time and place, in a world. They were to be related to him and to each other by a state of joyous knowledge; they were to derive from him and from each other; and he was to deign to derive his flesh from them. All this sprang, superfluous, out of his original intention —superfluous to himself and his direct purpose, not superfluous to his indirect purpose of love. It was to be a web of simultaneous interchange of good. 'In the sight of God', said the Lady Julian, 'all man is one man and one man is all man.'

This high creation came into existence; we have now the shadows, hints, and fractions of it for our instruction and encouragement. And that is all we have, except for the new work which was presently to follow. The original shone, in its proper glory, aware of its nature and of the nature of its lord. We cannot now make much of a guess at its nature, nor whether (for example) it was sequential in our sense; whether the Divine Birth was, in that state, in existence or still to be. The creation must presumably have been related to time in order that derivation (as between children and parents) should take place at all. But whether its only consciousness was of what we may call 'time' may be doubted; simultaneity may also have been known. To know simultaneity is not, of itself, to know eternity; that is a different matter altogether.

Its occasion, root, and centre was the Incarnation; that was the cause of it and the reason for it. The operation of the Holy Ghost was at once over the world and in the womb. It was a free generosity of love that deigned to create both the world and the secret womb; neither were necessary to his existence in flesh. But it was a generosity which perfectly foresaw (to talk in terms of time) the future, both for himself and for his creation. It would perhaps be more accurate to say that all was certainly then present to him, as it presumably could not be to the creation. But one cannot talk of it in those terms. It is our first intellectual descent from heaven; we are compelled to use terms which we know are inaccurate. Saint Paul gave us a new vocabulary, and the great doctors have continued the work. Theology, like all sciences, has its own proper language, but even the theologians are always sliding back into a one-sided use of that language. Their terms ought to be ambiguous; they ought to carry meanings at once in time and outside time. It cannot be done; and if it cannot among those experts, it certainly cannot among lesser creatures. So one is compelled to talk of God foreseeing and God determining, of pure Act as divisible, of eternity as altering, of perfection as becoming.

It is therefore that we are driven to speak of the Creation and the Redemption as separate acts and even separate ideas; as if Bridges's phrase of 'a divine fiasco' was obscurely justified. Even so intelligent a mind failed to grasp the very conditions of thought upon such things :

'For I reckon it among the unimaginables//how Saint Thomas, with all his honesty and keen thought . . .//should with open eyes have accepted for main premiss//the myth of a divine fiasco, on which to assure//the wisdom of God: leading to a foregone conclusion//of illachrymable logic.'

But certainly alteration there was. The possibility of alteration had been created as an element in the whole. That web of diagrammatized glory, of honourable beauty, of changing and interchanging adoration, depended for its perfection on two things—the will of God to sustain its being and its own will to be so sustained. He made—if we call it obedience we make the joy too dull (since we have, except at our momentary best and in our transient illuminations, lost the joy of obedience)—he made let us say the delight of a perfect response to his initiative a part of the working of the web. We could not otherwise become at once perfect servitude and perfect freedom. They are one and interchangeable, at least in consciousness: even now, in some states of love, it is possible at once to delight in being bound and to delight in being free. As Blake said: 'Contraries are not negations.' Much less there. In this world they tend to become opposites; that too perhaps is the result of what then happened.

But what did happen? The web depended on its exchanged

derivation, which itself sprang from the fact not only that all derived from him but also that he had ordained that he, in his flesh, would derive from all. The two derivations were, in him, a single act; and in that act, free and yet bound, bound by its free choice, all lay. Somewhere, somehow, the web loosed itself from its centre—also by its free choice. It chose; and it chose, in our phrase, wrongfully. What and how it chose we do not know. It may have been, literally, greed—some silly thing like a fruit; our own experience shows us how often the greatest spiritual decisions depend on something almost equally trivial—money or sexual pleasure. It may have been some other silly thing like pride—say, the belief that it could and would produce the divine Child of its own energy, an intoxication with its own powers, a worship of its own self. It may have been in this sense a dark mystery precisely of the birth of Christ.

But also it may have been what is described as being in the old myth of Genesis. I may perhaps be permitted to quote here what I have written elsewhere of that great myth:

'The nature of the Fall—both while possible and when actual—is clearly defined. The "fruit of the tree" is to bring an increase of knowledge. That increase, however, is, and is desired as being, of a particular kind. It is not merely to know more, but to know in another method. It is primarily the advance (if it can be so called) from knowing good to knowing good and evil; it is (secondarily) the knowing "as gods". A certain knowledge was, by its nature, confined to divine beings. Its communication to man would be, by its nature, disastrous to man. The Adam had been created and were existing in a state of knowledge of good and nothing but good. They knew that there was some kind of alternative, and they knew that the rejection of the alternative was part of their relation to the Omnipotence that created them. That relation was part of the good they enjoyed. But they knew also that the knowledge in the Omnipotence was greater than their own; they understood that in some way it knew "evil".

'It was, in future ages, declared by Aquinas that it was of the nature of God to know all possibilities, and to determine which possibility should become fact. "God would not know good

122

things perfectly, unless he also knew evil things . . . for, since evil is not of itself knowable, forasmuch as 'evil is the privation of good', as Augustine says (*Confess.* iii, 7), therefore evil can neither be defined nor known except by good." Things which are not and never will be he knows "not by vision", as he does all things that are, or will be, "but by simple intelligence". It is therefore part of that knowledge that he should understand good in its deprivation, the identity of heaven in its opposite identity of hell, but without "approbation", without calling it into being at all.

'It was not so possible for man, and the myth is the tale of that impossibility. However solemn and intellectual the exposition of the act sounds, the act itself is simple enough. It is easy for us now, after the terrible and prolonged habit of mankind; it was not, perhaps, very difficult then—as easy as picking a fruit from a tree. It was merely to wish to know an antagonism in the good, to find out what the good would be like if a contradiction were introduced into it. Man desired to know schism in the universe. It was a knowledge reserved to God; man had been warned that he could not bear it—"in the day that thou eatest thereof thou shalt surely die". A serpentine subtlety overwhelmed that statement with a grander promise—"Ye shall be as gods, knowing good and evil". Unfortunately to be as gods meant, for the Adam, to die, for to know evil, for them, was to know it not by pure intelligence but by experience. It was, precisely, to experience the opposite of good, that is the deprivation of the good, the slow destruction of the good, and of themselves with the good.

'The Adam were permitted to achieve this knowledge if they wished; they did so wish. Some possibility of opposite action there must be if there is to be any relation between different wills. Freewill is a thing incomprehensible to the logical mind, and perhaps not very often possible to the human spirit. The glasses of water which we are so often assured that we can or can not drink do not really refract light on the problem. "*Nihil sumus nisi voluntates,*" said Augustine, but the thing we fundamentally are is not easily known. Will is rather a thing we may choose to become than a thing we already possess—except so far as we can a little choose to choose, a little will to will. The Adam, with more will, exercised will in the myth. They knew good; they wished to know good and evil. Since there was not—since there never has been and never will be—anything else than the good to know, they knew good as antagonism. All difference consists in the mode of knowledge. They had what they wanted. That they did not like it when they got it does not alter the fact that they certainly got it.'

So much for the actual choice in itself. But the making of that choice may have been single or multitudinous. We know so little of that high state which haunts us for ever in our exile, and makes that exile preferable to us, and terrifies rather than encourages us with the hope of our return; it is not in mortal affairs alone that we can speak of 'hope that is unwilling to be fed'—we know so little of it that its conditions are unimaginable. But I have wondered if indeed we were not all there, if all mankind was not then simultaneous and co-inherent, and whether all mankind did not then choose amiss. It would not, in fact, be more astonishing than that one should; or the choice of one may, in fact, have wrecked all. But Adam may have been our name as well as our single father's, we in him and he in us in a state other than sequence. We were in him for we were he. We were all there, and we were all greedy or proud or curious. The original sin was in us as we originally were. The co-inherent will of mankind moved, and moved against its divine Original, which is the definition, so far, of sin.

Either then, we, ourselves, were in that state and there chose indeed;[1] or—as this has been the more common doctrine in the Church—the state of man's co-inherence was then so intense that the whole original body was desperately affected by the act of its primal member. The description of the new creation in the Epistle to the Ephesians is, reversed, a description of the Fall: 'that we . . . may grow up into him in all things, which is the head, even Christ: From whom the whole body fitly joined together and compacted by that which every joint supplieth,

---

[1] I do not mean to involve a prenatal existence. The choice is of another kind.

The Sin of Adam

according to the effectual working in the measure of every part, maketh increase of the body unto the edifying of itself in love.' 'That we may grow away from him all in things . . . the whole body disjoined and decompacted . . . decreases . . .'—The body was dissolved, or dissolved as far as could be, by the too-effectual working of that which every joint supplied.

The word 'body' there was not only metaphorical. The principle of the Incarnation had been a unity of God and Man in the flesh; and the principle of the creation had therefore been a unity of man—soul and body—in flesh. The physical body belonged to the category of the virtues, as everything did. We have, except for the poets, rather lost this sense of the body; we have not only despised it too much, but we have not admired it enough. There is a phrase in Wordsworth's *Prelude* (Book VIII, ll. 279–81) which defines it. Speaking of the Shepherds whom he has seen among the hills, he says:

> *The human form*
> *To me became an index of delight,*
> *Of grace and honour, power and worthiness.*

The operative word there is *index*. The body is there seen as an index to those holy qualities which we call Virtues. It is true we have largely lost the capacity of understanding the references in the index; in the whole great volume of our nature we do not know to which page the entries in the index, the references in the body, properly allude. We can remark sometimes in the love-poets something of the same sort, as when Dante talks in the *Convivio* of the mouth of the Lady of the Window, or Shakespeare of how love accentuates 'the functions and the offices' of the body, or Patmore says that in the body

> *Every least part*
> *Astonish'd hears*
> *And sweet replies to some like region of the spheres.*

But we do not all of us take the love-poets seriously. Wordsworth however was not (in that particular sense) in love with the Shepherds, and it is he who uses the word *index*. I do not propose

125

here to discuss the whole matter; it must be sufficient to say that on this interpretation the body is in one category what the soul is in another. The Lady Julian of Norwich said that: 'In the self-same point that our soul is made sensual, in the selfsame point is the City of God ordained to him from without beginning'—a not dissimilar maxim. The body was made as the physical formula of the Virtues, and whenever our eyes are opened we clearly perceive it to be so.

But then the chief name of all that balance and interchange and union of the Virtues in flesh was Chastity; for Chastity was precisely the name of its union with the Incarnation. Monks or married people, hermits or lovers, had this rule in whatever variation because of that union. Chastity is the obedience to and the relation with the adorable central body. It usually sounds to us now (let it be admitted) something of a negative virtue. That is false. It is the result of the Fall, after which, in the process of knowing good as evil, all virtues were bound, both in their physical and spiritual categories, to be understood rather by their positive denials than by their positive affirmations: even sometimes by their vicious opposites rather than by themselves. To suffer the Fall in this sense is what we had, and have, to expect. 'But in the beginning it was not so.' 'It is usual to interpret this "beginning" as a matter of temporal succession and to see no more in it than an indication of the order of sequence of events. . . . This "beginning" imports rather a divine principle of life.'[1] The principle of the relation of the created nature towards the Creator in that beginning is named Chastity; it is the natural relation in the beginning and the supernatural now. The imagination of this is what fills the word; it is not our quiet and chilling fancies that should limit it. The glory of the Divine Word itself is its chastity; the glory of the word 'chastity' is the reflection of the Divine Word. We have been taught that it is the principle of what we mean by celestial immortality; which

---

[1] Sergius Bulgakov, *The Wisdom of God*. I am not here claiming more agreement with the book than the quotation implies. 'The position is familiar,' but I do not remember to have seen it so clearly asserted before.

is union with the Word in terms of everlastingness as 'eternity' is union in the terms of uncreated simultaneity. Milton, in *Comus*, defined it so for all English verse and for all English attention, though indeed attention is the last thing we have given to the great speech of the Elder Brother, in that masque and ballet of 'divine philosophy'.[1] There he speaks of chastity as that quality which immortalizes the flesh. But the phrase—

> *turns it by degrees to the soul's essence*
> *Till all be made immortal——*

implies perhaps too much alteration on the part of the holy flesh which was dragged down with the will but which was not itself the origin of the Fall, since initiative could only act by the assent of the will.

Chastity then is part of that charity which (we have been taught) is the fulfilling of the law. It is the love of the soul for God. The other part of that charity is courtesy, which is the love of the soul for its created companions. 'On these two commandments hang all the law and the prophets.' They are complementary; nay, they are one. Chastity is courtesy towards God; courtesy is chastity towards men. The practice of the single virtue is named differently only in order that we may the more adequately enter into those divine secrets which it is our business to restore. It is this single virtue which was lost by the Fall; or say the two were lost—chastity and courtesy. They were lost in both body and soul, and the breach between body and soul, the breach in the indivisible, was fully established. The great physical ratification of that breach was Death. Whether something like Death —some change, some conversion—existed before the Fall we cannot know. But the Bible is full of suggestions that Death, as we do know it, is a result of the Fall. It is an outrage; it is a necessary outrage. It is a schism between those two great cate-

[1] It has been pointed out to me that the masque usually involved a dance, and that Milton for the actual dance substituted a philosophical. The suggestion is so much in accord with the high gaiety of *Comus* that I wish I had thought of it myself. The physical nature of the dance passes into the intellectual measure and there maintains itself in the sound of the verse.

gories of physical and spiritual which formed the declaration in
unity of one identity. Sin had come into the great co-inherent
web of humanity; say rather that all the web burst into sin, and
broke or was antagonized within itself; knot against knot, and
each filament everywhere countercharged within itself. It broke?
alas, no; it could not break unless its maker consented that it
should and he would not consent; his goodwill towards it (we are
assured) was too great. He loved it; he had loved it in the making and loved it made; and like any mortal lover he would not
consent that his wife should cease to love him. He would not
consent that she should go; that is, as between him and her, that
she should cease to exist; that is, in this only case, that she should
absolutely cease to exist. Death, and the second death, might be
the result; he was not to be moved. No; she had turned from him;
she had attempted to deracinate her life; but he was still her root,
and she should still have at her disposal all that he had given
her; she should still have life. Intolerable charity!

Sin then had come in. But what then is sin? It is easier to talk
about, to preach about, to rebuke, perhaps even to repent, than
to understand. Man had in some way determined to be greedy or
curious or proud, and this was an 'offence' to God. The grand
web had wished to know evil and it did. But in what sense could
this be an 'offence' to its Creator? Is the Lord more like our
fallen selves than we had supposed? Is he also proud and greedy,
and therefore in the worst sense jealous? Envious, by definition,
he can hardly be. But can that divine Other be credited even with
our virtues? We are continuously asked by the little books to
consider, for example, how horrible gluttony and fornication are
to the 'holiness' of the Lord. We are to look at 'God's awful
purity'; and when at any rate we look at the phrase, it seems
completely meaningless. How can God be 'pure'? How can our
lasciviousness kindle, as we are told it does, his 'wrath'? I have
spoken above of the 'generosity' of love; but again, strictly considered, how can Omnipotence be generous or Omniscience
wise? He laid commandments on us; we disobey; very well, is
he to be angry? Obviously not, unless he chooses that he shall;
all his motions are his will. If one created (if one could and

dared) two blackbeetles, and bade them copulate only on Tues-
days and they did it on Thursday, would one be 'angry' with
them unless one chose? Make the command as rational as one
can; suppose one had made them only capable of happy copula-
tion once in seven days, and they hurt themselves by disobedience—even then, would one be *angry*? Still less, he; unless indeed it is supposed to be part of his nature to permit himself the
infinite indulgence of superior spite.

But it will be said that nowadays we do not think in those
terms. It is not God who is 'angry'; it is we who have set ourselves in such a relation to him that we can only know him as a
fire and a hostility. The Judgement has been reduced from a
supernatural to a natural thing; it is the moral law within and
not the moral law without which is our test. Certainly if the first
sin were to know good as evil then this is credible, for it is precisely knowing our own good as evil. If men were determined to
know that, then it was that which they must know. So to abolish
the spectacular Judgement, however, does not help much. 'It is
he who made us, and not we ourselves.' The awful responsibility
of the First Cause remains with the First Cause. The great Saint
Thomas laid down that since God's dignity is infinite, therefore
an offence against it must be infinite in guilt, and demand infinite
punishment. But part of that infinite dignity was to create and
sustain; he sustains therefore in hell that he may so avenge himself? Supernatural judgement or natural sequence, we return to
the single cry that goes up against the Creator; it is but one
variation on one theme: that he did create, that he was the First
Cause.

Yes: but that creation had been after a particular manner.
That act which is called the Fall was an act by a being who had
not (in a sense) only been created. He *had* been created, of
course, but according to a special order which involved the non-
created. He was 'in flesh', or rather he was flesh at least as much
as anything else. He was the only rational creature so made, and
his flesh was in unique relationship to the sublime flesh which
was the unity of God with matter. The Incarnation was the
single dominating fact, and to that all flesh was related. The self-

communicated Joy of that was to be an all-communicated joy. It was related to all. The Fall therefore was not an affair which would necessarily leave the central and glorious Body unaffected. The angels were different. They might rebel and their rebellion be only in relation to God as Creator. In that sense, spirit as they might be, those celestial and splendid beings were wholly different from their Maker. But on earth it was not so. The Incarnation was the Original from which the lesser living human images derived. It was to be, if it was not already, intimately connected with their flesh; for it was to derive—since he had so decreed—from their flesh; if indeed it did not already in their simultaneity so derive. He had determined to be born of a mother, and that she also should be born of hers; and that physical relations of blood should unite him with all men and women that were or were to be. The Fall therefore took place in a nature which was as close as that to his own incarnate Nature.

To talk of God being in a dilemma is not only heretical but flagrantly silly: God is not like that. But it may perhaps be said that, when he created those superfluous beings of joy, he knew what they would do for to his eternity they were already doing it. He might, therefore, to borrow a word from the Old Testament writers, have 'repented himself'—had he allowed himself repentance. He might have abolished mankind. It had had its moment, its chance of co-inherent glory; it had refused it; let it go. Actually he 'might' not because he did not. But let the imbecile phrase stand; it does at least express the dilemma in which our understanding is placed. He might, but he did not. He might have abolished mankind and still, uniquely, have been flesh; he might indeed have been flesh through the uniquely preserved immaculacy of his mother alone, or with such others of her companions as he predestinated to be saved from that falling co-inherence into a sustained co-inherence with his mother and with himself. He did not. He preserved his original purpose, as he had known, from the beginning, he would.

What then? This was the intolerable charity of which we are speaking. Mankind had devoted itself to an egotism which meant destruction, incoherence, and hell. He would not let it cease to

The Sin of Adam

exist. But then the result was that if he was to submit to the choice of man, he was indeed to submit to that choice. He was not merely to put up with it as a Creator, he was to endure it as a Victim. Whatever sin was, it was a thing repugnant to his nature as Man, repugnant to his flesh; that was, in fact, its definition. Whether it was greed or pride or envy, it was still that which the Divine Word, in the limits he desired to set upon his earthly existence, would not permit himself to will. He derived, in his flesh, from men and women; but also in that ꞏ Incarnation he derived from his Father wholly and from his Father's will. Man had chosen an opposite behaviour. Greed or envy or pride, it was opposed to the nature and movement—yes, even the physical movement—of God in flesh. God in flesh was to maintain both incarnation and creation; he must then be the Victim of the choice of man. But why maintain it? there is but one answer—for love. Intolerable charity indeed—but now also intolerable for himself. Indeed, it killed him.

It is this love which has been the continual astonishment of Christianity, to others and to itself. It is this capacity and will in himself—in himself absolutely—of love towards his superfluous creatures which has seemed strange and adorable to that creation so thrown 'out of the pale of love'. But the pale itself is adoration, and wherever adoration exists the pale of love is recovered. It is everywhere strange also, within or without the pale, but the strangeness within is different from the strangeness without. Without it may be called a miracle; within, it is a marvel. That which had been new in and from the beginning determined now to be new also in another manner without losing the old. It was not to be only as a Victim that he subjected himself to the choice of his creatures. He accepted the terms of the creation whom he had limited his omnipotence to create; in that sense he accepted justice. If he meant to sustain his creatures in the pain to which they were reduced, at least he also gave himself up to that pain. The First Cause was responsible for them; he accepted responsibility and endured equality.

Creator and Victim then: the third function went with those two. He would not only endure; he would renew; that is, accept-

131

ing their act he would set up new relations with them on the basis of that act. In their victimization, and therefore in his, he proposed to effect an escape from that victimization. They had refused the co-inherence of the original creation, and had become (literally) incoherent in their suffering. He proposed to make those sufferings themselves co-inherent in him, and therefore to reintroduce them into the principle which was he. The Incarnation was to be a Redemption as well. He became flesh for our sakes as well as his own. In this sense all that has ever been said about his condescension was true. He 'condescended' to be involved intimately in acts so repugnant to his nature that, could they have been brought to a victorious ultimate conclusion, they must have destroyed that nature. Prevented from that by the stability of his divine nature, they would inevitably destroy their authors. Prevented from that by his sustaining power, they must eat into the life that was he.

He was indeed the actual life; or at least the life that was his gift to that human superfluity came under his government and resisted the Fall. Our whole fundamental mode of existence was divine. Man, rejecting him, rejected also the natural life. It is not perhaps going too far to say that, in that too-fatal hour, men and women were set against such simple things as breathing, as their original body and blood. Our physical nature was dragged down with our spiritual and laboured, as it labours still, in a state it was never meant to endure. The Incarnacy was to redeem the flesh from what it had not invoked as well as the soul from what it had. But at least our flesh again and again supports the Redemption; it bears witness to glories; it flashes now and then with the heaven to which it is native; and the great compact of Virtues, the physical formula of beatitude, exiled from its unity, yearns—and more innocently than the soul—for its original joy.

Creator, Victim, and Redeemer then. But how would the sin fare? Sin is the name of a certain relationship between man and God. When it is fixed, if it is, into a final state, he gives it other names; he calls it *hell* and *damnation*. But if man were to be restored, what was to happen to the sin? He had a name for that relationship too; like a second Adam indeed he named the beasts

132

The Sin of Adam

of our nature as they wandered in the ruined Paradise; he called this 'forgiveness'. 'Thy sins are forgiven thee; go in peace.' One of the greatest poets has shown us what he understood that word 'forgiveness' to mean in human terms. But what did the inventor of the word, since he was the inventor of the thing, mean by it? Something at least by which the sin was to be brought into perfect accord with the original good, the incoherence into the co-inherence, the opening hell into the opened heaven. Nothing else, obviously, would serve, for that, simply, was what had to be done. Continuing inflexibly upon the lines he had laid down for himself, he proceeded to do it.

CHAPTER IV

The Offering of Blood

It is always possible to read the Gospels with our minds on one particular element in the unique person of the God-Man. New meanings present themselves in relation to the whole when certain phrases are studied with respect to a part, to our Lord as Love, as Power, as Will. It seems possible therefore to consider his life, or rather the records of it, in relation to him as Forgiveness.

It is, from our present point of view, not yet at all certain what the word means. All that we take for granted is that the Trinity had determined the Incarnation of the Word, that They had determined and caused the creation of superfluous mankind with a purpose of entire joy, that mankind had set itself in such a relation to Them and especially to the flesh of the Word that it was bound, if the creation so ordained continued, to victimize its Creator, and that They had accepted that result and had determined that the original Incarnation should be a Redemption also; that is, that his life on earth should redeem life and earth. He was to be born, as he had willed, of a Mother.

The song in which the father of the Precursor, filled by Them with the divine Vision, praised the coming Thing asserted this. The Precursor was to prophesy and prepare for the coming of the Lord as the coming of salvation 'in the remission of their sins'. God's 'heart of mercy' (as the marginalia of the Revised Version calls it) was to be that in which the day shone upon those 'in darkness and in the shadow of death'. By the vision which appeared to Saint Joseph while he was meditating on the nature of justice-in-love the same promise was given: 'That which is conceived in her is of the Holy Ghost . . . she shall bring forth a son . . . it is he that shall save his people from their sins.' There was indeed something peculiarly applicable in the prophecy at that moment. For Saint Joseph 'being a righteous man and not willing to make her a public example, was minded to put her away privily'. If indeed the princely saint—so young perhaps and perhaps so in love—believing that he had been in some sense 'wronged' or at least deceived, desired no bitterness and no open declaration of resentment, but a privy hiding of a privy guilt, he had fulfilled much; he had set a great example to Christendom; he had acted as became all that was until that holy thing was born.

For before we come to the consideration of that holy Thing, it is perhaps worth while to look a little at what else had been. The present writer is incapable of discussing the matter of pardon among savages and aboriginal folk. There is, it seems, among many of them penitence, confession, and reunion with the society or with the god—and there are rites to that effect. The question whether these are to be held as imperfect representations of the Christian centre, or whether Christianity is to be held merely as a more intellectual, and even philosophical, development of those rites, is a question which has been discussed almost since Christianity appeared and seems likely to be discussed as long as Christianity—or any opposition to Christianity—remains. It depends so much on the *parti pris* that there is in fact little use in the discussion. It is one of the great advantages (or disadvantages) of Christianity that in the last resort it has no arguments; it can do nothing but say, in the phrase which the Church claims that she only has the right and power to borrow from her Lord: 'I am'. If indeed the existence of God were certainly probable to human reason—but it cannot be; at best, we cannot admit more than a reasonable likelihood. Faith is another kind of thing. Therefore the great disputes go on, and it is not impossible, though it rarely happens, that a man might accept by faith what his reason thought was unlikely. The split in our brain, as Siger of Brabant is said to have felt, is very deep. That does not do away with our duty to our brain.

The Forgiveness of Sins

That, however, is a digression. Anthropological discussion would be another digression. Whichever of the two above-mentioned alternatives is true, the main fact at present is the Christian decision. But before that was communicated—at least temporally—there existed the Jewish Law. This has been accepted by Christians, as a prelude to, and preparation for, the Christian; not so, naturally, by the Jews to whom it belongs. But there are two points upon which something should be said, (i) the three elements of the Law—moral, natural, ritual—and the matter of sacrifice; (ii) the prophetic idiom.

(i) The modern insistence on morals has caused to grow up a certain more or less defined suggestion that the moral element in the Law was of more value than the other. The Prophets, who particularly insisted on it, are regarded as being in some sense more advanced, even more 'spiritual', than the priestly schools with whom they are so often said to have found themselves in opposition. But (speaking without expert knowledge) there is in the original Law, as it is presented to us in the Canonical Writings no sign of this. 'Impurity' may be moral or ceremonial or natural. The real difference seems to have been that for the serious moral offences there was little chance of personal 'atonement'. The sentence continually is death—death for idolatry, death for witchcraft, death for incest, death for adultery, death for murder. Other, and many, moral laws are laid down, but there are few definite penalties attached to them. It is, obscurely, the blood that is involved, the blood that is important; one might almost say that wherever the blood is involved the Lord is involved. Even the killing of a beast without recognition of the Lord is made penal. 'What man soever there be of the house of Israel, that killeth an ox, or lamb, or goat, in the camp, or that killeth it out of the camp, and bringeth it not unto the door of the tabernacle of the congregation, to offer an offering unto the Lord before the tabernacle of the Lord; blood shall be imputed unto that man; he hath shed blood; and that man shall be cut off from among his people; to the end that the children of Israel may bring their sacrifices which they offer in the open field, even that they may bring them unto the Lord, unto the door of the tabernacle of the congregation, unto the priest, and offer them for peace offerings unto the Lord.'

This certainly is a ceremonial more than a moral uncleanness, and there seems to be some reason to suppose it was afterwards abrogated. The main point, however, is that, in most of the matters of uncleanness of any weight, blood was to be offered: the blood of the sinner or the blood of the sacrifice for the sinner, the blood in the place of judgement or the blood before the Mercy Seat. At the same time no member of that elect Society, 'the congregation of the children of Israel', was to eat anything with blood in it; 'the blood thereof, which is the life thereof, ye shall not eat'. 'I will even set my face against that soul that eateth blood, and will cut him off from among his people. For the life of the flesh is in the blood: and I have given it to you upon the altar to make an atonement for your souls: for it is the blood that maketh an atonement for the soul. Therefore I said unto the children of Israel, No soul of you shall eat blood, neither shall any stranger that sojourneth among you eat blood.'

Whoever ate the blood of an animal was to be cut off; whoever shed the blood of a man was to be cut off. The blood belonged to the Lord throughout all animals and all men; it was the life of the flesh and it made atonement for the soul. It was sprinkled before God for the soul, instead of the soul; that is, as a substitution for the soul. The expiation for the sins of the soul (since sin was necessarily of the soul) was by the life of the flesh, either by the flesh that was in union with the soul that had sinned or by some other. Man must not kill man; except by solemn decree as laid down in the Law or in war which was recognized by the Law. He might kill animals, but he must recognize their existence by recognizing the Creator of them; it was a permission and not a right.

The high Day of Atonement carried this idea to the innermost places. It was then that the two goats were to be chosen, the one to be sacrificed for a sin-offering, the other to be driven into the wilderness carrying the sins of the people. It was then that the high-priest was to go in to where the cloud on the mercy seat was interpenetrated with the glory of the Lord, and sprinkle with his finger seven times 'upon the mercy seat eastward' the blood of a bullock for himself and for his house, and afterwards the blood of the goat for the sins of the people 'because of the uncleanness of the children of Israel, and because of their transgressions in all their sins; and so shall he do for the tabernacle of the congregation, that remaineth among them in the midst of their uncleanness'.

The sprinkling of blood seven times from the high priest's finger before the mercy seat, where between the wings of the golden cherubim the Shekinah half-concealed and half-revealed itself in cloud, reduced the blood-offering to its most ritual and least visible form. But it did not alter the essence; that remained. The forgiveness of sins demanded it; without shedding of blood is no remission of sins. The suspension of sacrifice since the fall of the Temple leaves the Law still supreme; the decree is not altered in Israel. Nor elsewhere.

This ceremonial, because spiritual, importance of the blood, seems to apply generally. Almost any natural 'shedding of blood' is regarded as 'unclean'. Even surgical blood-shedding, unless perhaps it were confined to the priests, ought apparently to come under the same formal condemnation; not perhaps improperly, for it is, as the need for it is, a result of the Fall. A bleeding from the nose would be unclean. Yet war was permitted, and executions? They were permitted by the particular will of the Lord; they were permitted by the Law which determined what was permissible. The children of Israel only slew 'in the name of the Lord'. There is also, of course, that other great natural bloodshed common to half the human race—menstruation. That was unclean. But it is not impossible that that is an image, naturally, of the great bloodshed on Calvary, and perhaps, supernaturally, in relation to it. Women share the victimization of the blood; it is why, being the sacrifice so, they cannot be the priests. They are mothers and, in that special sense, victims; witnesses, in the body, to the suffering of the body, and the method of Redemption.

(ii) The idiom of the prophets is, as was said above, of another kind. There has everywhere tended to be a division, if not an actual conflict, between the prophets and the priests. It took place in Israel and outside Israel, and it has taken place in Christendom. What exactly the prophesyings in the early Church were we do not know. We do know that the organization of Christendom proceeded on sacerdotal lines, frequently opposed or complemented by prophetic outbreaks. Neither mode of religion is, it seems, entirely adequate without the other; neither can remain at its best without the help of the other. There must be something all but automatic, as there must be something anything but automatic. It is, of course, much easier to demand a prophet than a priest; and it is far, far easier to become a pseudo-prophet than a pseudo-priest. I will not say that almost anyone can be a priest; it would not be true for the priesthood is a vocation. But certainly almost anyone can imagine himself to be a prophet.

It has not pleased God to build either the congregation of Israel or the fellowship of the Church on prophets. They are the warning, the correction, the voice in the wilderness. Occasionally they occur in the ranks of the priesthood—Augustine is an example. It is often true that they recall the attention of the faithful to certain facts which are becoming blurred or forgotten. They trouble the customary ritual with a new sound. They are loved and hated at once, and both by good men. They pronounce, generally, the need of man to repent and be turned. It was this which was the overpowering note in the prophets of the Old Testament. Among the steady sacrifices and the habitual assemblies they asked passionately what, in fact, the pious worshippers were supposed to be doing: in the very midst, as it were, of the Temple courts, they cried out: 'Turn ye, turn ye; why will ye die?' In the very places where the convention of centuries slew and entreated and shook blood from its fingers, they declared that this also could be an evil and a danger of death. 'It is iniquity; even the solemn meeting.'

The phrase is so familiar that we have perhaps lost a sense of the terror. The Holy One, in the eyes of the prophets, was rejecting the means of reconciliation he had himself decreed; the Shekinah over the Mercy Seat shuddered back from the goats' blood that lay before it. But not for the sake of the goat. It is not the shedding of blood that is wrong; only its indecent, its unbecoming, shedding. When the same Isaiah cries out in the name of the Holy One: 'When ye make many prayers I will not hear; your hands are full of blood', it is repudiation of the blood of the sacrifice because of the blood on the hands that offer it. It is a too-easy interpretation that sees in the delighting-not in the blood 'of bullocks or of lambs or of he-goats' a more spiritual mode of approach. The prophet demands only what the Rite had already demanded—a repentance, a turning back to the Lord: 'Wash you; make you clean.' The furniture of the Temple had included the laver; cleansed hands were to sprinkle the ancient blood. But since the Law and the Rites had been formulated they had been forgotten—though the condition of the sacrifice was perennial and permanent. 'Thou shalt bring Aaron and his sons', ran the Law, 'unto the door of the tabernacle of the congregation, and wash them with water.' 'Wash you; make you clean', ran the new emphasis—but it was precisely a new emphasis on the old law. Bloody hands—hands stained with the blood of slain men, or guilty of blood thinned by slavery—were not fit to touch the sacrificial blood. It was precisely in the state of those fingers that the awful secret of obedience, of the accepted atonement, lay.

Yet there, though the hands were bloody with the life of men, lay still the single chance: 'though your sins be as scarlet, they shall be as white as snow; though they be red like crimson, they shall be as wool'. The congregation of Israel, the City of God, had carried on the old original idolatry; it had been apostate. 'How is the faithful city become an harlot! It was full of judgement; righteousness lodged in it; but now murderers.' It was to this renewed state of evil, in which even reconciliation had become iniquity, that the appeal of the High and Holy One was addressed: 'come now and let us reason together'. The Glory upon the Mercy Seat addressed itself to the double blasphemy before it; it exhibited the necessity of alteration, of obedience, of the good; it deigned to dispute with the sinner as it had not with the righteous man Job. The distinction is not unjustified. It is in the nature of man, as he knows himself, to demand an explanation, even a justification, from the Lord. But the state in which he can argue is not the state in which he repents; the conditions are different. No doubt the prophets of Israel were reasonable as the apologists of Christianity have been reasonable. But within the courts of reason lay the laver and the veil of the Holy of Holies; there things had to be *done*. The ministers of the Church should perhaps have been more sceptical and intelligent than they have altogether been; they should have practised, more than they have, the delicate incredulity which is the proper decency of the mind. If proof of this were needed, their history supplies it; the terrible history of the witch-persecutions, for example, when for lack of that incredulity a delirium of vengeance filled the Church and her ministers tortured the innocent as well as the guilty (if to torture an innocent man is indeed worse than to *torture*—to put to agonizing and continuous pain—a guilty man). But when this has been said, it remains that this applies only to the outer courts; the courtesies of love are not the kiss of the beloved. And the veil about the sanctuary is not the same as the things done within it.

There was expostulation for the sinner; there were only taunts for Job; the nearer to the centre the farther from an argument. Ezekiel himself did but renew the old bidding; he is one of the tenderest and most human of the prophets; he is full of lordly promises and of beauty, but the book called by his name ends with a description of 'the frame of a city', and in the city a house and in the house an altar, and the glory over it, but the blood of a young bullock sprinkled there. 'And the name of the city from that day shall be, The Lord is there.'

This union of the turning of the sinner with the offering for sin meant then the forgiveness of the sin. But what, even so, is the forgiveness of the sin? It is, in the prophets, generally its 'putting-away', a 'forgetting'. 'I am he that blotteth out thy transgressions . . . and will not remember thy sins'; 'I will remember their sins no more', the scarlet is to vanish, the crimson to die away. In the great healing and restoration which he has promised, the High and Holy One will set aside even the memory of the sin. This depends certainly on Israel's repentance; but once that is in process, the past is to be remembered no more. 'Behold, I create new heavens and a new earth: and the former shall not be remembered nor come into mind. But be ye glad and rejoice for ever in that which I create; for behold I create in Jerusalem a rejoicing and her people a joy.' The vision of a universal peace, and of the holy community restored is everywhere: 'a kingdom of priests, a holy nation'. The lordly passages in which that future is described are too well known to be quoted. They depend however on something like a hypothetical restoration of innocence; all the evil is to be removed; man, once he has repented, is to be treated as if he had not sinned.

Certainly the phrases so used of oblivion may stand for something else, for a seclusion into himself of the Lord's knowledge of the sin. The iniquity is to be covered in him. It must be admitted that in these passages there is very little allusion to the sacrificial 'propitiation'; and it is this perhaps which has helped to give the prophets their reputation for superior spirituality. The genius of Isaiah especially carries the similes and metaphors of the restored peace into an almost infinite sense of exalted natural goodness: 'they shall not labour in vain nor bring forth for trouble; for they are the seed of the blessed of the Lord, and their offspring with them. And it shall come to pass, before they call I will answer, and while they are yet speaking I will hear . . . they shall not hurt nor destroy in all my holy mountain, saith the Lord'. This is the image of the consummation and it is as good as any other image of that unthinkable state. But the effect of the removal of any allusion to the sacrifice is one of two things: either (i) the Lord himself has forgotten the sin; or (ii) only he remembers it, and that only to himself; his mercy is to spare his people the recollection.[1]

Speaking therefore very generally, we may say that in the Old

[1] There are, of course, the 'Suffering Servant' passages of Isaiah. But I have spoken of them in relation to the same theme in another place and do not wish to repeat the passage in this book. From our present point of view it makes little difference whether those few passages darkly foretold the Redeemer or not. The general tone of the prophet is, I think, as has been stated.

The Offering of Blood

Testament the Forgiveness is regarded in one of two ways. The sin (by definition) having been committed, the schism between God and men having (by definition) been opened, there remain judgement and mercy. The judgement is to leave the sinner to the sin, to the ruin and the exile and the pain. The Mercy operates in one of two ways, which are not exclusive and not, in the Old Testament, regarded as being exclusive, but are differently stressed in different parts. The first is the Rite of blood. It is not, so far as can be seen, very clearly explained, nor indeed could be. But the blood which is the life is to be offered as an atonement for the soul; and the blood of bullocks and goats is to be offered as a vicarious sacrifice instead of the blood of men. The whole burden of this approach is that without shedding of blood is no remission of sins.

The other way stresses something else. The very sacrifice of Reconciliation itself has, because of man's sin, become iniquity. 'He that killeth an ox is as if he slew a man; he that sacrificeth a lamb as if he cut off a dog's neck; he that offereth an oblation as if he offered swine's blood; he that burneth incense as if he blessed an idol. Yea, they have chosen their own ways, and their soul delighteth in their abominations.' The whole point of that passage is that the very substance of the sacrifice has been changed from clean to unclean. It is not consideration for the animals or disapproval of the blood that speaks; or what could be said about the dog or the pig? It is the Rite which has been turned into uncleanness. 'I also will choose their delusions'— one of the more appalling phrases of the Bible.

Or, even if the actual Rite has not been transformed, yet men use it without regard for the spiritual conversion that should accompany it. God cannot, or at least will not, put away man's sin unless man has put it away, or at least attempted to put it away. Social and individual iniquities make the Rite and the Pardon a delusion. 'I will choose their delusions'; I will agree that the Forgiveness shall be a delusion, that they shall think it has been and it shall not have been. From that still worse evil repentance nevertheless may yet save. Then the operating sacrifices shall continue; the blood of animals or (in those Servant passages of Isaiah) the blood of something other than animals is effective to the cleansing; and the knowledge is covered. It is covered from God's people, and it is covered either from God himself or in God himself. This is the offered covenant.

The blood on the altar and the seclusion of the sin to God— these then are the two points of the Old Testament: all that had been up to Saint Joseph and the Birth. Saint Joseph had precisely intended the seclusion. But that which now appeared on the earth was the original both of blood and seclusion. The Birth which now took place was of the body which was the Incarnation that had been intended from the beginning; and its blood was in its nature. The knowledge of the sins of men was that which, also from the beginning, had determined that the Incarnation should be a Redemption also. The Birth then into the outer world was a union of blood and knowledge. The priests and prophets had ordered the Rites and exhorted souls. But neither priest nor prophet knew what sin was; only God knew that, for only God knew what had happened when man preferred something alien to the nature both of the Godhead and the Manhood of the Incarnation. They had chosen delusions and he had consented, at the cost of his blood and his knowledge enduring the Delusion. He condescended therefore to be what had been intended, to be the child of a mother.

It has been the habit of Christendom to regard that mother with peculiar veneration; so much so that the Roman Church has declared, as a part of the Faith, that she was conceived immaculately, that is, without vestige of original sin, and very many non-Roman Christians either accept the same belief or would find no great difficulty in accepting it. It may, humbly, be supposed that so high, so original, a miracle had about it some such particular purpose as that his human affections should have no barrier to their direct operation. He who wished to exercise all human virtues would not be without the virtue of *pietas*; his Manhood venerated what his Godhead had sustained and saved, achieving (it is said) in the instant of her conception what he achieves, sooner or later, in all redeemed souls. There was in the Roman Church in the seventeenth century a particular devotion to the Heart of Jesus and Mary: the single word united the double devotion of love. There was, I suppose, between them nothing for either to forgive; yet on that unforgiving love all other loves depended. It is the only case in which the word can be used except with a sense of hardness; there it is even more tender than its opposite. Certainly that also has its meaning; it reminds us still of humility. Love that forgives, which is the only love we can, or can ever, know, is tender and beautiful; but Love that has nothing to forgive can be—I will not say, unconfined in any part, for confined love is not love, but—less characterized by the recollection of its opposite. The mystery of such a love is as unimaginable as our pre-fallen state; and the climax of matter depended on it. There sprang from it the very flash of Forgiveness. She who in the free exercise of her choice loved her Creator because he chose that she should, became the mother of his Incarnation, the mother therefore of his victimization and redemption.

He became then Forgiveness in flesh; he lived the life of Forgiveness. This undoubted fact serves as a reminder that Forgiveness is an act, and not a set of words. It is a thing to be *done*. It may be done easily or with difficulty, but there is only one alternative to its being done, and that is its *not* being done. It is as much a thing happening as a birth is. 'The spirit of forgiveness' is, no doubt, a beautiful thing, but it does not exist except in acts—at any rate, as far as we are concerned. The acts, in fact, especially when done with a certain sense of self-compulsion, are all we know of the spirit. The birth of Forgiveness was the birth of something of flesh and blood, of brain and bone. It appeared in the world at a certain time and place—in the world which we know as time and place. And it proceeded to live a life characterized (we are to believe) by acts and words which, in their relation to men throughout, were precisely Forgiveness. It exactly claimed this power, and it called it a power, an energy: 'that ye may know that the Son of Man hath power on earth to forgive sins'; 'thy sins be forgiven thee'. This ascription to himself is like the similar ascription to himself of powers not certainly to break the law, but certainly of some right to control it. He says, for instance, that the Son of Man is lord of the Sabbath, but that the Sabbath was made for man, and not man for the Sabbath. He identifies himself with man, but he never equalizes man with himself, and this is true of forgiveness also. He commands men to forgive debts owed to them, but in the parable as in the Lord's Prayer, that forgiveness depends on their own debts being forgiven. He declares it to be a source, but man is to use it as a measure. This indeed is the secret of all the difference: he does not measure himself by man but man by himself. He certainly is the identity but it is for man to discover him so. 'With what measure ye mete, it shall be measured to you again; good measure, pressed down and running over, shall men give into your bosom.' We can choose another measure than himself at our own risk. It is the assent of the Divine Son to the kind of measurement demanded by the rebel angels which Milton used to precede their overthrow.

> *Therefore to me their doom he hath assigned,*
> *That they may have their wish, to try with me*
> *In battle which the stronger proves, they all*
> *Or I alone against them, since by strength*
> *They measure all, of other excellence*
> *Not emulous, nor care who them excels;*
> *Nor other strife with them do I vouchsafe.*

CHAPTER V

Forgiveness in Man

There is no space here to study all the records of that Life in terms of Forgiveness, nor indeed could anything of the sort be properly done except after years of attention; the danger of the invention of neat morals and pretty metaphysics is too great. But certain incidents in that Life stand out. It was the Life that was the fact—of Forgiveness as of everything holy else, and there was no moment in that Life which was not, towards men and women, a fact of Forgiveness, or at least a fact of the offer of Forgiveness. It proceeded steadily towards the consummate Forgiveness and the consummate Reconciliation, but they were not apart from the Life.

The Temptation, for example, is precisely, among other things, a temptation of Forgiveness, an effort to turn Forgiveness into something other than itself. All temptations are, in a sense, the same; they all depend on the rousing of some false hope, and on some action for its satisfaction. The order of the three temptations in the Canonical Writings cannot be of first importance, or we should not have been given two different accounts; we may presumably use each for edification without denying the other. The first temptation of Forgiveness then is to procure, through its own operation, some immediate comfort. The stones—let us say, the stones of offence—which are in the way are to be turned at once into bread. They are to perform the office of bread and not of stones. No doubt something like this may eventually happen to the holy soul; no doubt, in the end, the very stones themselves become nourishing. The nourishment derived at last from that hard strong state which can be described as 'stones' may be found to be much superior to that easier appeasement of natural hunger described as 'bread'. Our natural hunger desires immediate comfort. Yet any haste after this comfort is apt to destroy the whole act of forgiveness. It may often be easier for us to forgive than not—easier because more comfortable; nor is it always wrong to do so, any more than it is wrong to eat bread. But to pretend to forgive for the sake of one's own comfort is nonsense. 'Man does not live by bread alone but by every word that proceedeth out of the mouth of God'; that is, by God's knowledge of sin and forgiveness. It may be possible to return to that point presently.

The Second Temptation, let us say, is the setting on the pinnacle of the Temple; this is the order in Saint Matthew. The principle of this is that the Son of God should 'tempt' God; that Forgiveness should presume on its own nature instead of referring all to God's will. It assumes that it will be sustained by the divine messengers; nay, it assumes that the divine messengers will be there to support *it*. Inconceivable as it may seem that the humanity of the Son of God should feel that temptation, yet we must believe that he did, or the whole thing is false. But for us this temptation is probably even more common than the first; the worse temptations are always the commonest. The first was a kind of Sloth; this is Pride. Pride is the besetting sin of Pardon, almost the infernal twin of Pardon; it is its consciousness; rather, say, its self-consciousness become its only consciousness. It is the condescension, the *de haut en bas* element, which is with so much difficulty refused. After all, if one has been injured, if one has suffered wrong? 'Cast thyself down,' the devil murmurs, 'the angels will support you; be noble and forgive. You will have done the Right Thing; you will have behaved better than the enemy.' So, perhaps; but it will not be the angels of heaven who will support that kind of consciousness, unless by a fresh reference of ourselves to Forgiveness. 'Thou shalt not tempt the Lord thy God.'

The Third Temptation is not perhaps so common. The false hope of comfort, the false hope of superiority; and now? The false hope of freedom, but a freedom given by the devil. Can

Forgiveness in Man

Forgiveness worship the devil? all the virtues can worship the devil. Was not the Incarnate tempted? and is one to suppose the temptation was not real? No; in some sense Forgiveness is promised the kingdoms of this world; and how? Precisely by being set free from grudges and resentments, from bitterness and strife. This certainly is the proper nature and the proper result of Forgiveness, but then also Forgiveness which *primarily* desired that would not be forgiveness at all. It is but the mere point of *whom* one adores, the very last point, so small, yet so much all. It is the 'having nothing yet possessing all things' of Saint Paul turned into a maxim of personal greed. If one could achieve that state one would be completely free, one would no longer be hurt by others. To be, or to desire to be, free from being hurt by others, is to be, or to desire to be, free from the co-inherence of all human souls, which it was the express intention of Christ to redeem. In the perfect redemption, no doubt we all shall be free so; and when all, then each one. But till all, none. The achievement would be exactly hell; it would be to desire something other than he. 'Thou shalt worship the Lord thy God and him only shalt thou serve.'

Such then were the temptations he rejected, the delusions he would not choose. He exhibited delusion as delusion; he left the Church to declare what delusion was. It has not done it, or it has; the discussions on its fidelity or apostacy need not detain us here. He himself exhibited the facts of existence. Neither comfort nor pride nor detachment were to interfere with them; if they did, the facts would combine with the delusions to bring about hell. Yet he restored what was permissible; the first of the marvellous works did but increase enjoyment. He did not merely give men wine; when they had already drunk wine, he gave them more and better wine. He who would not make bread for himself would make wine for others. 'Others he saved; himself he could not save.'

All this matter of the Temptation was, in our sacred Lord, after its own and central kind, and indeed must still remain so. No definition or dogma can explain to us how Forgiveness was tempted not to be Forgiveness, and Love not to be Love. We

The Forgiveness of Sins

only know that he maintained his exact function; he remained free. He remained free, that is, to proclaim forgiveness—free to derive that power from his Father, free to exercise it towards us. When he had returned to his public life he began to do so: notably, in the case of the man sick of the palsy. It was one of those occasions on which he definitely declared that the miracle was a sign of something else. It will be remembered that the sick man had been lowered through the roof by his bearers; and the narrative proceeds: 'And when he saw their faith [not, for whatever the distinction is worth, his alone, if his at all], he said unto him, Man, thy sins are forgiven thee. And the scribes and Pharisees began to reason, saying, Who is this which speaketh blasphemies? Who can forgive sins, but God alone? But when Jesus perceived their thoughts, he answering said unto them, What reason ye in your hearts? Whether is easier to say, Thy sins be forgiven thee; or to say, Rise up and walk? But that ye may know that the Son of man hath power upon earth to forgive sins (he said unto the sick of the palsy), I say unto thee, Arise, and take up thy couch, and go unto thy house. And immediately he rose up before them, and took up that whereon he lay, and departed to his own house, glorifying God. And they were all amazed, and they glorified God, and were filled with fear, saying, We have seen strange things to-day.'

The 'strange things' were the double renovation of power— the sign that the sins are forgiven is the healing of the palsy. The proclamation is of a fact, a fact coming after another fact, that of faith; and out of this strangeness spring amazement and glorifying and holy awe. The record reads not altogether unlike certain moments of experience in our own lives—directly religious or indirectly religious; the moment of the vision, one way or another, of power. It is a matter for some consideration whether we do not often fail to grasp that power, whether we lose (if we do) the effect of renovation, precisely because we do not afterwards root our experience in the forgiveness of our sins. The Glory appears, but we can only belong to it by virtue of being united to it as a whole; that is, by the evil as by the good; by sins as by virtues. It is the movement of sin towards it which is called repentance; it is the movement of the good towards it which is called faith. The consciousness of repentance—that is, the consciousness of sin in love; that is, of the forgiveness of sin—is the preservation of humility; it is the glass in which we can see darkly something of that great virtue which we can never see in itself.

The 'strange things' were the reunion of the sick of the palsy, physically and spiritually, with the Glory of God. It was a renovation of spirit and flesh, and all the rest of the Gospels is like it, for all the rest is the account of the Glory so united or of the means of the uniting or of the rejection of the uniting. It comes as a renewal of nature as well as of supernature; it changes water into wine for those who have already drunk wine, and multiplies food for those who are in need of food. It comes 'eating and drinking'; it is even denounced as 'a gluttonous man and a winebibber'. It is no longer, as it had been under the Jewish Law, a hidden thing; the proclamation of the kingdom was that everything should be known. All—'every secret thing'—is to be brought out into clarity. It is in this clarity and charity, between men as between God and men, that 'the high dignity and neverceasing perpetuity of our nature' consists. One thing alone he hid, as it were, from his exhibition of himself in his kingdom, the mysterious sin against the Holy Ghost. As there had been a possibility of disobedience in the original creation, as there had been a possibility of iniquity in the Rites of the Jewish Law, so there was a possibility of final rejection in this restored creation. There was still an obscene outrage which man might insist on finding and choosing; he hinted and hid it.

And what then was the forgiveness of which this was the power? It has been greatly described by William Law.[1]

'What is God's forgiving sinful man? It is nothing else in its whole nature but God's making him righteous again. There is no other forgiveness of sin but being made free from it. Therefore, the compassionate love of God that forgives sin is no other than God's love of his own righteousness, for the sake of which and through the love of which he makes man righteous again. This is

[1] Stephen Hobhouse, *Selected Writings of William Law*, Letter IV.

the one righteousness of God that is rigorous, that makes no abatements, that must be satisfied, must be fulfilled in every creature that is to have communion with him. And this righteousness that is thus rigorous is nothing else but the unalterable purity and perfection of the divine love which, from eternity to eternity, can love nothing but its own righteousness, can will nothing but its own goodness, and therefore can will nothing towards fallen man but the return of his lost goodness by a new birth of the divine life in him, which is the true forgiveness of sins. For what is the sinful state of man? It is nothing else but the loss of that divine nature which cannot commit sin; therefore, the forgiving man's sin is, in the truth and reality of it, nothing else but the revival of that nature in man which, being born of God, sinneth not.'

This is what he lived; what was the conclusion of the life? It is very well known; it is the crucifixion of the power to forgive. Certainly, the enemies of Christ did not realize it as that; it was indeed their reason for rejecting him, or one of their reasons for rejecting, that he claimed that power and proclamation. They declared that none could forgive sins but God alone. He also declared the same thing; he referred that, as he referred all, to his Father. The agreement on principle was complete; all controversy was on the question of the authority of Christ to declare what he also declared he did not, so far, originate. He declared himself to be its voice, its operation; they asserted that he was its contradiction, and a blasphemy. The dispute remains. Either he was indeed that Forgiveness in action or he improperly arrogated to himself that deific annunciation. It may be observed that it was a thing he never asked from men—he who was continually proclaiming his own humility. He taught men to forgive each other; he made it a necessity of the kingdom; he withdrew hope from those who would not understand that necessity. But he never suggested that he himself should be forgiven—by any man or any god; he assumed, lucidly and wholly, that there was nothing to forgive and none who could forgive. Nor did he ever quite forgive. He never did say: 'I forgive you.' He who talked of himself continually never spoke of himself in that. He said:

Forgiveness in Man

'Father, forgive . . .' All the sin was elsewhere; all the penitence must be elsewhere; all the pardon was elsewhere. God forgave; he declared forgiveness; men were to be forgiven.

He concentrated upon himself the two ideas which had marked the Jewish tradition. Sins had been forgiven by virtue of the blood; 'it is the blood that maketh atonement for the soul'. The result of that atonement had been the seclusion of the knowledge of the sin into God. The angelic glories of heaven had proclaimed before the birth of Jesus that he had come to save his people from their sins; he himself declared that he had come to die: 'the Son of Man *must* . . .' His agelong victimization was perfected. It had been of old a cause for denunciation of the faithful by the prophets that they had defiled with non-sacrificial blood the altar of the sacrificial; that the solemn meeting had been made iniquity and that the Rites had become obscene. The new Rite was indeed hidden. None upon earth (unless indeed the Divine Mother—but there is nothing to show it, and something against it)—none upon earth knew that the awful and unique Rite was in process of presentation. It was secluded within his own knowledge alone. But it was a closer union than any the ancient Law had known or decreed. For this was not only the blood of the sacrifice making atonement for the original sin; it was the insulted sacrifice still making atonement for itself. Doubly misused, it was doubly powerful. Its power was in itself; the sacrifice sacrificed itself. 'It was in his power', said Augustine, 'to be affected in this or that way ôr not.' In the old Rites the blood of the offering and the consequent forgiveness had been separate things; their connection had been, or rather had seemed, almost arbitrary. It may be, because of it, that the whole animal creation has indeed a greater place than we know; the feast of the Holy Innocents ought perhaps to be thought to include those calves and goats and bulls who died, unknowingly, too soon, and, unknowingly, for vicarious satisfaction. They were symbolical? alas, they were living! they were of less value? we owe them still their own; they were sacrificed by command of the Will? it may be that the Will recollects them, and it was not perhaps without reason that it was forbidden to the faithful of the Old Dispensation to eat the blood; it was not safe until their Maker had also given us his. If that great Feast of the children who also did not will to die, and did not know for whom they died, and yet have been canonized because of that ignorant death—if that feast cannot be extended to include the sacrificed beasts, then it might not be altogether a useless act of devotion to God if the Church recollected before him one day in the year the irrational innocents who also died. He certainly whose sacred blood was not without relationship to theirs may have recollected them when he concluded their blood with his own, when the veil of the temple, behind which the mystery was wrought, was at last rent; and all was exposed— sin and repentance and sacrifice and pardon.

He substituted then his knowledge for their ignorance; his full consciousness for their partial; his reason for their unreason. The Forgiveness became the sacrifice. It is worth while to consider that precisely the Forgiveness was then—must one say *endangered*? How else—if at all his temptation and his trial were real? In some sense, that must be true which can only be expressed by saying that the possibility of his Redemption *might* have been an impossibility. He *might* have chosen, at any moment, not to continue; he *might* have prayed for the twelve legions of angels; he *might*, in fact, have descended from the cross, before he was deposed thence. But these things are for the theologians; it is sufficient here to note only (however it be phrased) that possible impossibility. Or, if we must not say even so much, yet at least it is worth while to contemplate for a moment the entire disappearance and negation of Forgiveness. That, after all, was what his slayers were, unknowingly, about. For the best of motives or the worst, or in some confusion between (but, for reasons given elsewhere, I would rather think the best), they were engaged in the entire destruction of Forgiveness. The atonement of the Temple was being contradicted by their purpose in this new Rite as it was being fulfilled by his purpose in the Rite. Forgiveness between God and man, and forgiveness therefore between man and man, would, had they had their way, have ceased upon earth.

Contemplate for a moment the result. We underrate the

things which, under the Mercy, are still natural to us; much more, in all the religions, supernatural; much more, in the Christian Church, final. Man remembers his ancient co-inherence still; it is not to say he need, nor that he often enough does. But reconciliation is still recollected and present even in a pagan world, in our own culture or in others. The removal of reconciliation would have left us, quite simply, unreconciled, and that everywhere and not alone in religion. The present state of international anguish would have been universal, and that not only among nations. Every grudge and every resentment would have lasted; the dream of anything else would have been but a dream, and a less recurrent dream. The possibility of love would have depended upon the lack of offence; and no mortal lover but knows how easy offence is. The least rudeness would have rankled, and the very idea of anything else would have disappeared. We should have come to depend upon resentment; therefore, upon hate; therefore, on vengeance. This, which spreads fast enough even now, would then have spread with less and less difficulty and less and less delay. War, in the house and in the field, secret or open, malicious and continual, would have been our doom; there would, simply, have been no alternative. We could never have forgiven our children nor our children us; they would have been born into a world of malice, and their malice, had they survived, would have been directed against us. It is true they probably would not have survived; their parents would have loathed them too soon and too well; and, indeed, remove but that habit of reconciliation, and the begetting of children would soon have ceased. Sterile and stupid, the generations of men would have hastened into hell.

Such was the shadow of the great darkness over the cross, which lingers a little when the darkness is over and the Death alone is present. The suspension of his life allows us a space to consider it, but the nightmare ends with his Return. But his Return was from something other than nightmare. 'His agony', wrote Law again, 'was His entrance into the last eternal terrors of the lost soul, into the real horrors of that dreadful eternal death which man unredeemed must have died into when he left this world. We are therefore not to consider our Lord's death upon the Cross as only the death of that mortal body which was nailed to it, but we are to look upon Him with wounded hearts, as fixed and fastened in the state of that twofold death, which was due to the fallen nature, out of which He could not come till He could say "It is finished; Father, into thy hands I commend my spirit."'

It was in this state that he forgave: forgave? say, he loved and renewed those who had brought him into it; he loved them so as to maintain them while they brought him into it, as he had maintained the tree that made the wood and the metal that made the nails. He forgave from the state of 'the eternal terrors of the lost soul'. He so forgave that he exchanged his love for man's loss; he received the loss and gave the love. It is the mere nature of forgiveness; there can be no other; but then it was there, and therefore everywhere; it is its nature—yes, but then its nature does so exist. No less, in our degree, will serve as our duty; no less—unbearable glory!—is the true nature of our very life. But whatever distress his glory lays upon us in our present state, it cannot be anything like his state then nor as bad as our only alternative state. On the other hand, when he returned, he returned with his scars. The Resurrection is something other than the spiritual survival. It is the continuation of the physical in the highest degree; the continuation of the past into the present. But the past was now exposed. His glory secluded the scars no more; therefore it did not seclude the sin that led to them. The blood had been shed; it had made atonement; but it was no longer to be lost, unnoticeably, like that of bulls and goats had been. It was, as the great scene with Saint Thomas Didymus shows, and as the legend of Saint Martin of Tours maintains, to be recollected for ever in the stigmata whence it had flowed. He revealed himself, at that time, obscurely, only to those who already knew him; the rest of mankind had yet to learn to know. It is his method always.

The Resurrection was the Resurrection of Forgiveness, but the sin which brought it about was no longer to be covered, even by and in God himself. He became an energy of forgiveness in

the Church. He had stated the principle in the years of his life—
almost, as it were, by accident, as an answer to a question or a
clause in a prayer. That principle was that the active and passive
modes of forgiveness were not to be separated; that they were
indeed, in some sense, identical; one could not exist without the
other. This was not a matter of language; it was a fact, a law of
nature—anyhow, of redeemed nature. To forgive and to be forgiven were one thing. 'And forgive us our sins as we forgive
them that trespass against us.' This was the entreaty and this
was the answer to the entreaty. The comment on it had been in
the parable of the Wicked Servant. The parable is not perhaps
altogether consistent with our feelings; it may shock us that a
man who has had his debts forgiven should have them again set
against him. But the moral and metaphysical doctrine is exact;
this is what happens. It is that state of things in action which the
Lord's Prayer entreats to come into action. The threat implicit in
that prayer—in that single clause—is very high; it is the only
clause which carries a threat, but there it is clear. No word in
English carries a greater possibility of terror than the little word
'as' in that clause; it is the measuring rod of the heavenly City,
and the knot of the new union. But also it is the key of hell and
the knife that cuts the knot of union.

The condition of forgiving then is to be forgiven; the condition of being forgiven is to forgive. The two conditions are coexistent; they are indeed the very point of coexistence, the root
of the new union, the beginning of the recovery of the co-inherence in which all creation had begun. Out of that point of double
submission the City of God was to rise. Double submission? Yes,
for in this the active was to be as submissive as the passive. The
disciple had to be forgiven; he had also to forgive—both in
obedience to the command of this Figure which was itself Forgiveness. The Figure was, and pronounced, a state of things; it
was the new situation of man. That which Immanuel alone was,
he alone could not passively experience. He expressed the prerogative of pardon; he could not submit to its necessity. Both prerogative and necessity were to be promulgated through the
disciple. Our Lord conceded the new prerogative to the freewill

already conceded at the creation. There had, then, been no need for it; there was, now, every need for it. Men could forgive each other by the same freewill which, since the Fall, had been used for injuring each other. But the concession was also a command, as all the Divine concessions are; it is not in the nature of God to concede possibilities of the first order which may be left unused. 'Everyone which is perfect shall be as his Master', and perfection being the only thing he required, the disciple was to forgive, of his own choice, as well as, of his own choice, to be forgiven. The single Will acted in him in a double mode—and the disciple had only to obey. One might be agreeable and the other not, or they might both be agreeable, or neither; that was of no importance. As in the Morning Joy and the Evening Joy, the individual, and, indeed, the whole world, opened out into the forgiveness asked from it, and turned to close again in the forgiveness granted to it—and these two were one.

Such was the single fundamental of the Church. The Church was the new world; into the Church the whole old world was to be drawn. Anyone who was not rooted in that fundamental simply did not belong to the Church at all; except again by new faith in that power of promulgation and by new repentance for having failed from that power. At first indeed the Church even doubted this. It was not, for some time, at all clear that there could be repentance and pardon after baptism. But it became tender in the end, as the great dialogue between Christ and Peter had taught it to be. Yet its tenderness was compulsive; if there was to be no end to the operation on the divine side, nor was there to be on the human. 'Seven times? ... seventy times seven' —in a day, in an hour, in a moment. As in old days the iniquity of the solemn meeting was itself a subject for repentance, so now was any failure of forgiveness. The disciple might not achieve perfection, but he must mean perfection, so only would Immanuel achieve perfection in him. Without that he was not even a disciple; he was, by necessity, self-outcast. But with that he was able 'to provoke unto love and good works', and to be provoked. The second is perhaps even more difficult than the first; the consciousness of having been forgiven is almost the only condition in which one can endure that provocation.

This then was the temper, the *ethos*, of the Church. The opposite temper, the alternative *ethos*, was expressed in the dulcet words: 'With what measure ye mete, it shall be measured to you again; good measure, pressed down and running over. . . .' The sentence certainly covers both: measurement there certainly must be. Love is measurement in detail, as all good things are. Love is the smallest, and yet the most important, detail in the whole measurement of the universe. The exactitude of the measurement was the same anyhow; 'no idle word' was to escape it. Everything was to be known; God had secluded in himself so long as he himself remained secluded. But now he had been exposed and exhibited—by his will, in flesh and birth; by man's will, in the death of flesh. The exposition of himself meant the exposition of all that was in himself—including the sin and the sacrifice he had deigned to become.

CHAPTER VI

The Technique of Pardon

Yet, it may be said, forgiveness itself had to be measured, that is, to be understood; and it may be suggested in answer that there are three chief modes in which we do understand it in its own high and lofty style. The virtues, owing to the laborious detail in which they have to be pursued by us (and we can only pursue them in laborious detail—'general good', said Blake, 'is the plea of the scoundrel, hypocrite, and flatterer')—the virtues are apt to be subdued to our own niggling style. But in themselves they are not so; they are gay and princely; and so they are seen when they are recognized in others simply because we are in a state of love towards others. We can admire them in their freedom in others when in ourselves they must seem, if not in servitude, at least only just escaped from servitude, sore from the manacles, bleeding from their effort at freedom, lame, purblind, unheavenly. It is our business to admire them heavenly whenever they can be so seen; the opportunity is in such states as marriage and friendship, and we do very well to take it whenever it is found. 'This ought ye to have done, and not to have left the other undone.' We must not cease from our own labour because the glory is seen free in another; but neither must we cease to admire the glory because the labour is all that we can feel in ourselves. Nevertheless we might unconsciously learn to carry even grace with an air; it is not ours, and so we may; we have nothing to be proud of; another has laboured and we are entered into his labour. An unconscious magnificence of any virtue is only to be attained by the practice of that virtue combined with humility. Since this is

160

bound to be conscious, it is not always easy to achieve its opposite; but in itself the grace of 'the weight of glory' is precisely its lightness.

It may be suggested therefore that forgiveness can be considered as applicable in three ways: (i) to things which need not be forgiven; (ii) to things which can be forgiven; (iii) to things which cannot be forgiven. The first and the third, put so, are contradictory; nevertheless, the phrases may for the present stand.

(i) Things which need not be forgiven. There is a tendency among some Christians to make a burden of things which non-Christians would pass over lightly. They overdo forgiveness as they overdo patience and other virtues. No doubt Christianity and life ought to be one; no doubt, essentially, they *are* one; that is why we are at odds with both, because we are still often at odds with that which is the root of both. No doubt we ought to be always looking for opportunities of leading the Christian life. But there are two ways of doing even that—one is with courtesy and the other without courtesy. Courtesy is our whole business towards our neighbours; it is indeed spiritual self-preservation; well, but then so is love. Love, we have been told, is slow to anger; it is, as a result, slow to forgive, for it will not be in a hurry to assume that there is anything to forgive; and if there is, it will not be in a hurry to make a business of forgiving. Many lives are passed without the experience of anything in others which can seriously be supposed to need forgiveness, though not indeed without themselves committing wrongs which may seem to need forgiveness. I do not mean here only that we should not make an exterior fuss; we should not even make an interior fuss. The good manners of the City of God are supernaturally instinctive; the instinct of the new life should warn us of any approaching danger of pomposity or guile, and the danger is subtle. The new way—forgiveness, humility, clarity, charity—is there; it is the old man on the new way who is the tempter, and who beguiles us away from it while we think we are walking on it. We cannot, and need not, when we seem to be insulted or injured, be unaware of it; but we can dismiss the awareness with a shrug or a smile—at ourselves. 'A sense of humour' has been over-praised; wit would be better, could we attain it, but it must be a whole and healthy wit, and it should be but an instrument at first. Love 'doth not behave itself unseemly'; that is, it carries itself beautifully; it takes no need to itself. An awareness of injury, unless it has been deeply aimed at the heart, is exactly taking heed to oneself; an awareness of forgiveness, unless it is asked, is apt to be a taking heed to itself. Not to be quick to forgive in this sense is as much a part of the divine command as not to be slow is in another; we have to be free; even from the virtues, in the end.

(ii) Things which can be forgiven. But how then to distinguish, to carry ourselves handsomely, to avoid rejoicing in iniquity? Rejoicing in other people's iniquity, one way or another, is a not uncommon fault. There is at least one simple distinction, even if it cannot always be used; it lies in the request for forgiveness. Saint Peter, in the dialogue with Immanuel mentioned earlier, included this as a condition, and our Lord permitted it: 'if my brother sin against me and turn again?' The question here is of serious, but not fatal, harm; injuries which wound but do not kill the heart; blows which might be returned in anger but not with a cold and determined vengeance; such wounds as leave love, where it is felt, still felt as in being. We may be permitted perhaps to take the term 'my brother' as significant there; at least, for the present purpose. Say, that the consciousness of brotherhood, of relationship, is still vital; it is within that relationship that the harm has been done. It is then within that relationship that the forgiveness must exist, and since all relationship must thrive or decay by what it holds within it, by its elements, it is from such forgiveness that the relationship must thrive. But then, since mutual love thrives from mutual acts, the forgiveness must be a mutual act, an act of agreement. Love, indeed, in that sense, is mutuality; the effort to practise love is an effort to become mutual; that is where it goes beyond what is generally called 'unselfishness'. To prefer another's will to one's own is much, but to become another's will by means of one's own is more, and is indeed the necessary thing for love. 'Love', said

The Technique of Pardon

Saint Thomas, 'is nothing else than the willing of good' to the beloved; and when the functions of the beloved are exercised in the good, there one must love the beloved in his or her functions; one must will those functions, and be a power towards them. The union of lovers is in that double energy. It is true indeed that he is unwise who falls into the pseudo-romantic illusion of saying: 'O I can only do it *if* . . .'; who demands companionship before he can be industrious and love before he can be chaste. 'They only can do it with you who can do it without you.' But, that being so, there can be an added power; as it were, the oxygen to the mountain-climber. No doubt, if one cylinder were not there, another would serve; there is nothing sacrosanct about oneself; anything might do as well. But if one is required to be oxygen, one had better be oxygen.

This where and as it applies. In some things it does not apply. Thus the most intense physical form of mutuality is, normally, in intercourse between the sexes; the most perfected, there, that which results in childbirth. But the physical form is but one, and not, for all the mystery of the body, in the end the most important. Many separated lovers have discovered that. Of the spiritual functions, the realization of a sense of sin is one, and of repentance, and of pardon. A double energy should go to it. This is not to say that it is the lover's business to impose a sense of sin on, or to demand it from, the beloved; he would be a fool who was thus rash; more especially he would be a fool who did so without a great and piercing sense of exchange. Guilt is in all; it is the guilty who forgives. Entreated to forgive, by another as guilty, it is his whole duty to restore reconciliation by any and every means, for ever and ever, without condition. The protested single guilt on the part of another leads more easily to a sense of one's own single guilt; therefore to a sharing of the condition of guilt. The entreaty for forgiveness does not, among mortal creatures, abolish the sin, but it does a little transform it. It transforms it doubly; it provokes a shy humility on the part not only of the pardoned but of the pardoner. The awful consciousness (in any serious matter) that he is necessarily exercising, in his proper degree, the conceded prerogative of Christ,

163

prevents pride, prevents anything but shame. Must the lecherous forgive the malicious ? the slothful the arrogant ? it seems no less. But not, surely, without a keener sense of lechery or sloth, a renewed entreaty on his own part, a confessed exchange of guilt. Not perhaps, vocally, then and there; it is sometimes a solecism to intrude one's own sins, though hardly to remember them secretly.

'The falling out of faithful friends renewing is of love'; the old poem has a deeper sense than perhaps it altogether meant. The word 'faithful' certainly has. The mutual operation is an operation of 'faith'; it is a further entering into 'the substance of things hoped for', a further exhibition of 'the evidence of things not seen'. It may be objected that such operations, in many and many a relationship of love, are purely 'natural'; they neither invoke, nor think of invoking, the supernatural world of which Saint Paul was thinking. So; but then the great goods do operate naturally. Where there is love, there is Christ; where there is human reconciliation, there is the Church. To say so is not in any way to weaken the supernatural: where the consciousness of that exists, the power of the operation ought in every way to pierce deeper, to last longer, to live stronger, than in the natural. The invocation of Immanuel is at the root of all, and where the invocation is conscious the consciousness of love should be greater. 'Ought' . . . 'should' . . . it is staringly obvious that in our present age it does not. The children of this world are even now in that other wiser than the children of light. And indeed for many of us it is the natural passion of love rather than the supernatural principle which directs and encourages us. This is well enough; it is more than well; so long as we intend to pursue the natural into the more-than-natural of which it is a part. The real distinction between Christians and non-Christians is here, as always, something very like the risk of hell. He who professes a supernatural validity for his virtuous acts must follow them out into that whole validity. He who professes only nature may be rewarded with the best of nature, perhaps with more than nature; he who professes more than nature, if he does not practise it, may be left with neither. 'Unto him that hath shall be given;

from him that hath not shall be taken away even that which he seemeth to have.'

It is in relation to the next heading that the dependence of the natural on the supernatural can be again raised.

(iii) Things which cannot be forgiven. The phrase is only humanly true, and (everything considered) it is perhaps not even that. It would be dangerous to say that there is any princely goodness of which the human spirit is not capable; its original derivation beats in it still, and its divine kinship moves still in brain and blood. A perfection of pardon is not only a Christian dream. But it is, if not only, yet certainly, a Christian doctrine. Whether a pagan ought to forgive all injuries may depend on his own knowledge of spirit, on his 'inner light'. But it depends on no such unsure thing in a Christian; it depends on the will of Christ and the doctrine of the Church. The Christian has no doubt of his duty, though he may have every difficulty in fulfilling it. He is not, in that, very different from the faithful of other great religions; the Buddhist is a recipient of the same spiritual command. The difference between them, in that, is of another order. Forgiveness of all injuries is demanded of the Christian because of the nature of our Lord, and it is demanded entirely. The phrase 'things that cannot be forgiven' is therefore to him intellectually meaningless. But it may in fact mean a good deal all the same. It is true that few of us are, fortunately, in a position to understand that meaning; no injuries of which the forgiveness seems unbelievable have ever been done us. But probably there are at the present moment more persons alive in Europe than for many generations to whom such injuries have been done. The forgiveness of the poor—even if a casual and pagan pardon; say, rather, the lack of resentment in the poor— we have had always with us, little though we have cared to understand it. But the massacres, the tortures, and the slavery, which have appeared in Europe of late have impressed themselves upon us. In the ruined houses of Rotterdam—or indeed of England—among the oppressed thousands of Poland, there are those to whom the phrase 'things that cannot be forgiven' has a fearful meaning. Must they nevertheless be forgiven? they must.

The Forgiveness of Sins

Must vengeance, must even resentment, be put off? it must. There is certainly a distinction between the desire for private vengeance and the execution of public justice. But there is no excuse for concealing private vengeance under the disguise of public justice. The establishment of tribunals to impose penalties for breach of treaty-agreements is, I suppose, possible; how much more, if anything, may be either possible or desirable we need not here discuss. It would have nothing to do with its main theme; and indeed of that main theme Rotterdam and Poland are only contemporary and spectacular examples, chosen for convenience. The injury done to many in that kind of war is greater than the injury done to one in private, but the result, from a Christian point of view, cannot be other. That must be, everywhere and always, the renewal of love. But in such a state as we are now considering, that renewal of love means little less than heroic sanctity. It is upon such heroic sanctities that the Church depends—depends in the sense that they are its rule, its energy, and its great examples. It is less likely, when the hurt is so deep, that there will be any request for forgiveness. The deeper the injury, the less inclined the evildoer is to ask, even to desire, that the sin may be forgiven—perhaps the less able. Remorse rather than repentance—with all that repentance means—is likely to exist; there is already present the possibility of that kind of half-anger, half-anguish which is too easily built up into a continued wickedness, a separate hell.

The depth of vengeance on one side; on the other, at best remorse, at worst persistence in injury—can these be turned into the reconciliation of love? It is at least in such states of all but everlasting conflict that the Church expects the coming of peace, and that she demands, on the side of the injured, the heroic sanctity of pardon, or the interior preparation for it. In itself it may not properly exist until an opportunity is given it by the request; it cannot be mutual till then; therefore it cannot, in itself, *be* till then. But the whole passion of it must be there, waiting for the second's opportunity; the spirit waiting for the letter, without which it cannot perfectly be. And here again it is to be maintained that, even in such difficult moments, the double responsibility of guilt enters; sinner to sinner. Heroic sanctity is required perhaps to forgive, but *not* to forgive is ordinary sin. There is no alternative; the greatness of the injury cannot supply that. It becomes—an excuse? no, a temptation: the greater the injury, the greater the temptation; the more excusable the sin, the no less sin.

It was said at the beginning of this book that it was impossible to write such a book; and besides the impossibility of the theme, here is a side impossibility. Can any writer lay down such rules, for himself and for others—especially for others? No; and yet without those rules, without that appalling diagram of integrity, there can be no understanding, however small, of the nature of the interchange of love. For on the achievement in the extreme all depends. The courtesies of our first division, the intimacies of the second, spring only from the truth that the fact of forgiveness is absolute. Immanuel, by his existence in flesh, by his victimization, by his life as forgiveness, and by his proclamation of forgiveness, showed it as absolute. In doctrine and in action, the Church maintains the fact.

There are two footnotes, as it were, which should be added to the consideration of all three divisions. The first might be called the Rule of the Second Step. In matters of forgiveness, as in all other virtues (and some vices) the first step is comparatively simple compared to the second. Hell is always waiting for the rebound. The only prevention of the rebound is perseverance. The first moment of forgiveness is nearly always confused with other things—with affection, with delight, with honour, with pride, with love of power; some good, some bad, all distracting. It will happen, often enough, that the forgiveness is rather an emanation of these things than a power in itself. But then, directly afterwards, the good elements will withdraw themselves, and leave the reconciliation to its own serious energy; and if that energy is too weak, it will break; but it will not break alone, for the affection and the joy will be hurt too. Or else the evil elements, the pride and the sense of power, will dominate the reconciliation, and it will become egotistical and a false illusion of the good. Even the light courtesies and settings-aside of our first division need sometimes a second shrug: nothing is achieved at once.

> *The horse is taught his manage, and no star*
> *Of wildest course but treads back his own steps;*
> *For the spent hurricane the air provides*
> *As fierce a successor; the tide retreats*
> *But to return out of its hiding-place*
> *In the great deep; all things have second birth.*

The virtues, however wild their course, have to tread back their own steps; they have, young and innocent, to be taught their manage. They have to learn to be always ready when they are called on; so, they may in time, but only in time, be ready without the calling; their obedience to time and place in us sets them there outside those conditions in the end: 'servitude and freedom are one and interchangeable'.

It is in relation to this management that the second footnote may be useful: a footnote on recollection. There are two methods of reconciliation: that which remembers the injury in love and that which forgets the injury in love. It is a delicate technique of pardon which can distinguish and (without self-consciousness) use either. Either may be desirable here and now, though there can, of course, be no question which is finally desirable and even necessary to the existence of the Blessed City. There (its architect told us and all its architecture maintains) all things are to be known. We had better not forget it; but even so, 'he that believeth shall not make haste'. Oblivion—say, perfect seclusion of the injury in God—is often here a safer means. It is often likely that to remember the injury would lead only to some opposite injury. Even the best-intentioned Christians are not always at ease in these sublime states. The mutual act of forgiveness can, too often and too quickly, become a single memory of the sin; the single memory a monstrous interior repetition of recollection; the monstrosity a boredom; the boredom a burden. Or, worse, the sense of superiority is too easily involved. We may say and think we have forgiven and then find we have not; or, worse again, think we have forgiven, and in that self-decep-

168

tion *never* find that we have not; we may die supposing ourselves to be kindly and self-pleasingly and virtuously reconciled—'And then will I profess unto them, I never knew you; depart from me, ye that work iniquity'. But also we may in fact have forgiven— say, half-forgiven; and the pardon is thought to free the pardoner to every claim and compel the pardoned to every obedience. '*Such*', wrote Blake,

> *Such is the Forgiveness of the Gods, the Moral Virtues of the*
> *Heathen, whose tender Mercies are Cruelty. But Jehovah's*
> *Salvation*
> *Is without Money and without Price, in the Continual Forgive-*
> *ness of Sins,*
> *In the Perpetual Mutual Sacrifice in Great Eternity: for behold,*
> *There is none that liveth and sinneth not.*

If it is forbidden to us to demand as a condition of our forgiveness any promise that the offence shall not be repeated, if when he conceded to us the declaration of reconciled love, God retained that condition to himself alone, how much more is it forbidden us to make any other claims, to expect an extra kindness, to ask for an extra indulgence. And how all but impossible to avoid! Forgiving or forgiven, we can claim nothing, at the same time that we have, in God, a right to claim everything. Conceding the permission to promulgate, he conceded also the right to demand; in the Church such things happen. In sacramental confession itself it is the priest who (conditions fulfilled) cannot refuse absolution. Nor we forgiveness; the sinner has all the advantages, as the just son of the prodigal's father felt. But, so admitting, we can slide into an evil mutuality: how easy to claim consideration in return; or if not to claim, at least to expect; or if not to expect, at least to feel we have a right to—somewhere, somehow, *some* right! Alas, none but what our injurer, of free choice, gives us. Otherwise, the mutuality itself becomes diseased; it grows corrupt with the dreadful stench of the old man on the new way. To forget the sin is the safer method.

Yet oblivion too has its dangers. The beauty of the joyous and mutual interchange is bound to dwindle a little if the occasion is put aside; that is, between lovers. And in those other more austere instances, where love exists not as a strong and conscious affection, but only as a deliberate act of the will—in Rotterdam and Poland, say—even there, though the soul can live from the wound of the heart, yet it is perhaps less easy to learn to do so if the hurt is put aside. Our derivation, our nourishment, is both from our sorrows and from our joys; it is so obvious, and so harsh and lengthy, a business to find it there. Say, Forget; and add, But do not say Forget. Love must carry itself beautifully; it must have style. It may seem absurd, in such high matters, to use so common a literary term, and yet there is hardly any word so useful. Style, in literature, is an individual thing. *Le style, c'est l'homme même*—style is the man himself, said the French maxim. Considering what men are, it need not be pressed too far. Yeats indeed declared that a poet's work was often the anti-type of his individual nature; he quoted Keats and Dante as examples. But in religion the problem hardly arises; in religion we are dealing with 'the man himself' and there can be no separation. His style is his particular manner of courtesy; his lack of style is his lack of courtesy. It may be sedate or glorious, distant or intimate, firm or even flamboyant. Only, if it exists at all, and to the level at which it exists, it will not be insincere or partial. A purity of virtue will do much; it cannot, in any one case, do all. What is needed in every case, in every virtue, in every act of every virtue, is that all purities of intention should be precisely there. Pardon is perhaps the act in which all are most needed; it is apt to grow false if any are missing; it is quite certain not, then or thereafter, to have its proper joy. It gathers up within itself all the powers of love, because in fact it is love—chaste with the glowing chastity of the Divine Son. Chastity is the spirit of which courtesy is the letter; the spirit waits for the letter and the letter for the spirit; both together are love—love in knowledge, which is the only kind of love with which the Christian Church has, finally, any concern.

It would sound absurd to say that pardon itself has, on earth and between men and women, to be pardoned. Yet some kind of occasional meditation on this might not be unwise. 'They feel most injured who have done the wrong'; and even if they repent and ask for forgiveness, they quite frequently begin to feel the forgiveness as an injury when they have it. It is not easy to be forgiven; certainly not to continue in the knowledge of being forgiven. Only the princeliest souls can bear it naturally for long; only the holiest supernaturally—by which word is meant there not the pardon of God for man, but the pardon of man for man in the Church. There will be something selfish in the pardon; that, at least, will be resented, if nothing more—improperly resented, no doubt, but then it is itself an impropriety. Our very forgiveness is an opportunity for us to be forgiven—by God, of course, but also, and with more tardiness, on our side and his, by our neighbour. We were both sinners, we were both guilty—yes, originally; but also we are both sinners and guilty in the very act of penitence and pardon. Let it rest; it is the very promise of life.

Such then is the relationship which is to be attempted among the redeemed; which is, by virtue of something else, to be achieved. The union of all citizens of the City is not to leave out any facts. Everything that has ever happened is to be a part of it, so far as men are strong enough to bear it; the holier the stronger. Everything that has ever happened is an act of love or an act against love. Acts of love unite the City; acts against love disunite. But of this disunity it is necessary that we should not be too quickly aware. The Lady Julian laid down a great maxim when she said: 'here was I learned that I should see my own sin, and not other men's sins, but if it may be for comfort and help of mine even-Christians'. The earthly courtesy which we discussed under the first of the three headings above is a heavenly courtesy also. It is opposed to courtesy in all its degrees that we should be too quick to cast out the mote.

At the same time not even the greatest courtesy is blind. Love itself, as we know from Love itself, is not blind. If the mote in our neighbour's eye leads him to murder another neighbour, we may presumably notice it. We are permitted to remark it when his mote leads him to take away our coat, though we are not then to insist on pulling it out; we are, on the contrary, to offer our cloak also. It has been said a hundred times that on those principles no organized State could exist. It is clear also that it is precisely on those principles that the Church is intended to exist, and does indeed exist; at least it has no others.

The transfiguration of the earthly State into the heavenly City is a work of the Holy Ghost. The word *transfiguration* there is apt; it is a change of diagram. It does not involve, as the Manichæans do vainly talk, a putting-off of the natural body, but it does involve that natural body itself becoming accustomed to a whole new set of laws—at first as commands, then as habits, last as instincts. It has often been pointed out that we use the word 'law' ambiguously; that the 'laws' of the Decalogue are not the same thing as the 'laws' of movement. The alteration of the one into the other, individually and generally, is the work of the Holy Spirit in the Church. It is an agelong work, and it has to be done individually—even the general work has to be done individually. Efforts have been made—not too successfully—to set up a Christian republic, a kind of Christian anarchy, in which the secular State with its laws and penalties should not exist. It is not merely from the greed or tyranny of the higher ecclesiastics that the Church has so often felt uneasy with even the most admirable State. The State, as it were, longs to stand still; but the Church cannot stand still. Her very name is speed; her Mind is set always on virtues so great, on modes of living so intense, that we cannot begin to imagine them. The most elementary images of them are repulsive to us—except at rare moments, and even then we are not sure. Can we order all our affairs by instincts we hardly begin to feel? to assert it and to deny it is alike dangerous. Must we, for example, consent that men, other men, shall be killed and maimed? The answer to that is simple—we must. We may do it by ourselves inflicting death and torment on others (by bombs or however), or we may do it by abandoning others to death and torment (in concentration camps or wherever), but one way or the other we have to consent by our mere acts. To call the one war and the other peace does not help. This —whichever it is—is certainly, in part, the result of what we do. Is there any direction? Even to quote 'Thou shalt not kill' does not finally help, for we have been taught that consciously to

abandon men to death is, in fact, to kill. To hate is to kill; to kill
is to kill; and to leave to be killed is to kill; yes, though (like the
lawyer in the Gospel) we do not know who our neighbour is.
There are wars to which that does not apply; there are wars to
which it does. Such is the dilemma in which we find ourselves;
and then what happens to forgiveness?

I have taken the most extreme example; but the root dilemma
is common enough. It is a dilemma in which any man existing in
an organized State is continually involved. Capital punishment,
the whole penal law, the instability of the poor, a hundred social
evils, are all part of it. To disagree with this and that no more
helps us—or very little more—than to agree. While we remain
part of the State we are involved in its life. Disagreeing leaves
us where we were; we might as well disagree with the Fall, as
no doubt most of us do. We cannot, so far, escape the nature of
man, the original and awful co-inherence of man with man in
which we were created. Certainly we must follow whichever
path our conscience, under the authority of the Church, indicates;
we must disagree with one and agree with one as we are instructed. But the moral burden is the same both ways.

What then are we to say, in this matter of forgiveness, about
the State, if anything? especially, if such a thing can indeed exist,
about the Christian State? Morally, of course, in the Christian
State, where its members were all Christians, the matter would
be simple in essence, though perhaps complex in operation. The
courts would operate in a parallel order to the confessionals—
only the confessions would be public. But that would certainly
involve repentance on the part of the guilty. Whether in a profoundly Christian State it would be possible for the Church to
produce a Guild of those who would vicariously bear the legal
penalties on the part of the confessed criminals, even perhaps to
the death penalty itself, if that were still imposed, is but a
dream. Yet only by operations that once seemed no less of
dreams has the Church reached its own present self-consciousness—by devotions not dissimilar, powers not otherwise practised. We do well to dream such things as long as our dreams are
in accord with the great Christian vision. This is only another

example of substitution, upon which our Lord created the original universe, and which he afterwards reintroduced in his own awful Person as the basis of his redeemed world. Pardon itself is an example of it; the injured bears the trouble of another's sin; he who is forgiven receives the freedom of another's love.

We shall have certainly to remake the State before such things can be; humanly speaking, we shall have almost to remake the Church. But then we can never quite talk of the Church 'humanly speaking', and the State we shall have to remake anyhow if it is to last and succeed even naturally. The bounty of the spirit then would be its freedom: our poverty can only rise into that bounty by the practice of such freedom as is found in a speed of giving and taking forgiveness.

'The State's function', it has been said, 'is inherently ambiguous, and in some ways resembles that of the Law in Saint Paul's theology.'[1] In the matter of the secular law that ambiguity is mostly to be discerned in the inevitable use of penalties. Punishments, under the State, are either retributive or reformatory. But either way they have to be enforced; they are put into operation by the decision and force of the magistrates very much against the will of the guilty. It is at least a question whether this, though our only method, is not from the fundamental Christian point of view a false method. The chief use of punishment in the State is to frighten the majority of citizens from behaving as they wish to behave, and as a minority do behave. But penance in the Church is not of this nature, nor is it retributive nor reformatory. It is much more in the nature of something undertaken, as a 'satisfaction', by the guilty and repentant person; it is, that is to say, *desired*. The idea of that state which is called 'purgatory' is not different. That certainly is purging, is reformatory; but it is not entirely without the notion of compensation. The mountain of purgatory, wrote Dante, 'shakes when some soul feels herself cleansed, and free to rise and mount. . . . Of that cleansing the will makes proof, which seizing the soul with surprise avails it to fly. It wills indeed earlier, but

[1] Canon O. C. Quick, *Christianity and Justice*.

174

is not then free from that desire which the divine justice, against the will, sets as once towards sin, so now to the torment.' The will to reach God is counteracted by the desire for the compensation of sin. But this is in the pardoned souls; they are pardoned before they are in purgatory; it is why they are in purgatory.

This flame towards both pardon and punishment is the mark then of the elect soul. It has its parallels in lower spheres. Lent, it has been said, is no such unjoyous season; many a mortal lover, guilty of some offence, sighs for a penalty; Shakespeare, as we saw, sealed it in Angelo—

> *Immediate sentence then, and sequent death,*
> *Is all the grace I beg.*

In such states penalties may be pronounced by authority; they are invoked by the subject. The submissive is not passive only; it is on fire with love; it hastens to experience the great balance of sin and punishment—the words separate too much what becomes a unity. But in the State punishment is bound to seem, at least partly, self-preservation. The community penalizes offenders in order that it may itself live. It is not so in happier states; there, it may be said, punishment is love-preservation, and only self-inflicted. It was in relation to sin and pain that the Lady Julian said: 'All shall be well, and all shall be well, and all manner of thing shall be well'. Certainly in small things this can be seen; it is in the greater that it is difficult. It is true that the same Lady said that all our life was penance, and perhaps the burden of life might be eased if it were taken that way. 'A kind soul hath no hell but sin.'

All this belongs to the place of division. But it points to the place of union. Forgiveness is the way to the state of union and first appreciation of the state of union. It is so that it is seen (to return to Shakespeare) in those concluding scenes of the plays which, more than many religious books, make the great human reconcilement credible. In that poetry it remains, as do so many of the experienced mysteries, a wholly human thing. It has been said of Shakespeare that he wrote the whole supernatural life in terms of the natural, and it is true that he is the great protagonist

175

of natural life without apparent need—humanly speaking—of the supernatural. It was a divine gift to us; he remains for ever a rebuke to the arrogant supernaturalists; they try to annex him, but it will not serve. He may or he may not have been religious in his personal life; he is not, when all is said, even when what has here been said about *Cymbeline* is said, religious in his poetry. But if anything of this nature could be deduced from his poetry the one thing that could be deduced would be that man's human nature was made on the same principles as his supernatural. He is, in that sense, as necessary to check the excesses of the disciples of Dante as Dante is to check the excesses of his disciples. Either without the other is incomplete; and it is not perhaps altogether by chance that Imogen and Beatrice are both the instruments and orators of pardon.

CHAPTER VII

Forgiveness and Reconciliation

The distinction, however, between the state of union to which forgiveness is a means and the opposite state is more extremely expressed in two other writers. The first of them is that admirable but heretical poet William Blake.[1] Forgiveness plays a great part both in the shorter poems and in those which go by the name of the *Prophetic Books*, especially the longest of them, called *Jerusalem*. This poem, like the other *Prophetic Books*, is concerned with the loves and wars, the destruction and salvation of great super-human beings. These beings pass from one kind of existence to another; from a world of life to a world of death, and again to a world of life. It is true we cannot be very much interested in those great forms themselves; they are not sufficiently clear for us to know or distinguish them, except after very careful study. But this is not so much incompetence on Blake's part as one might unwisely suppose. What he thought mattered was not 'individuals' but 'states'; it was these states of being which he desired to define and declare, and individuals in his verse—even his own giant individuals—are only there to reveal the states of being in which they exist. Poetically, this was no doubt a fault or at least a misfortune. The Divine Man in *Jerusalem* declares

I go forth to create
States to deliver Individuals evermore. Amen.

[1] I call Blake heretical for various reasons which cannot here be discussed. But I do so with some hesitation, since the explorations of his work which have been so far made have mostly been in the manner he denounced—by detached intellectual analysis. What might be found could a better method be discovered I do not think we know.

The Forgiveness of Sins

It cannot very well be done in verse, for it is only, on the whole, through the individuals that we know the states to which they belong. But it is true, on the other hand, that this way of thinking is, within proper limits, of great moral use to us. We normally tend to think of ourselves as *doing* something—as forgiving, as loving, as believing. Such a method of thought is perhaps all of which we are capable. But it is, as it were, wholly a doctrine of 'works'; the old hymn was not unjustified—

> *Lay thy deadly doing down;*
> *Doing ends in death.*

The life of 'faith' is preferable; 'faith' is the name given to an operation by which we are to become—become what? become the Reconciliation. This does not rule out the necessity of what was said before about acts; say, Do, and add, But do not do.

This passion of becoming was a great part of Blake's verse; his figures labour with it. For our present purpose the two opposite states which he described are 'vengeance' and 'forgiveness'. It might be argued that he too much ignores that idea of justice which is the root and effort of the State—or, not to confuse the word with two uses, let us say the Republic. The word Republic is, as everyone knows, derived from *res publica*, the public or common thing; and it is precisely this common thing which has been in question. It is this, and not the individual soul, which Christendom has taught us is, under the name of the Christ-in-the-Church, Christ the City,

> *the Eternal Vision, the Divine Similitude,*
> *In loves and tears of brothers, sisters, sons, fathers, and friends,*
> *Which if Man ceases to behold, he ceases to exist.*
> *. . . Our wars are wars of life and wounds of love,*
> *With intellectual spears and long winged arrows of thought.*

We may or may not suffer from exterior things; from this interior thing we must all suffer—or almost all. It is certainly possible that a few holy souls may have been born already so disposed to sanctity that their effort is natural and their growth instinctive; they move happily into goodness, and their regeneration seems to have been one with their generation; but even they may have suffered more than they chose or indeed were able to communicate. Their wounds were hidden; their sensitiveness bled privately; they appeased the rage of their companions in their own quietude, and no one has done more than envy a celsitude more painful than anyone knew. But for the rest of us, the 'wounds of love' mean a sudden or a lingering death. The second death itself is indeed but a choice in time; if we prefer it before our natural death, we are taught that it may be salvation; if after, that it may be eternal loss. The death of our Lord introduced that choice. He who died in his natural life brought into our natural life the possibility of the choice of a supernatural death and therefore of a supernatural life; this is the life of faith.

> *Wouldst thou love one who never died*
> *For thee, or ever die for one who had not died for thee?*
> *And if God dieth not for Man, and giveth not himself*
> *Eternally for Man, Man could not exist; for Man is Love*
> *As God is Love; every kindness to another is a little Death*
> *In the Divine Image, nor can Man exist but by Brotherhood.*

'Man is Love.' I do not remember the divine epigram elsewhere. It is this which is the original part of all our life; to divide it into natural and supernatural is a schism inevitable to us, but an inevitability only as a means to unite or disunite the common, the public thing. It is in our most private hearts that the Republic is established, but our private hearts can force themselves out of the Republic. We can refuse the maternity of Love, the protectorate of Grace: intolerable and too certain concession! and then ?

> *Hark! and Record the terrible wonder, that the Punisher*
> *Mingles with his Victim's Spectre, enslaved and tormented*
> *To him whom he has murder'd, bound in vengeance and enmity.*
> *Shudder not, but Write, and the hand of God will assist you.*

The Sinner is for ever justified? no; perhaps Blake was indeed heretical. Certainly the Republic is ambiguous, but the humanitarian terror of punishment will not be more than a Precursor, a Saint John Baptist there. It is the fashion nowadays among many

Christians to sneer at humanitarianism and liberalism (in the
political sense), and this is natural because of the undue trust that
has been reposed in them. But 'the lights of nature and faith',
wrote John Donne, 'are subordinate John Baptists to Christ';
humanitarianism is a formula of prophecy. Pity is still half a
pagan virtue; compassion a Christian. To forgive is indeed compassion, the suffering with another. To refuse to forgive is to
refuse that other as himself or herself; it is to prefer the spectre
of him, and to prefer a spectre is to be for ever lost.

> *All things are so constructed*
> *And builded by the Divine hand that the sinner shall always*
> *   escape;*
> *And he who takes vengeance alone is the criminal of Providence.*
> *O Albion! If thou takest vengeance, if thou revengest thy wrongs,*
> *Thou art for ever lost! What can I do to hinder the Sons*
> *Of Albion from taking vengeance or how shall I them persuade?*[1]

To say that the sinner shall always escape is a rash definition.
Our Lord did not say so. But he did say that even the collection
of our just human debts was a very dangerous business; he did
say that we were to pray to be forgiven *as*—precisely *as*—we forgive; he did say that the debts forgiven us reduced to nonsense
the debts owed to us. It is not therefore to read the New Testament too rashly to see in it rather more than a suggestion that,
as far as we humanly are concerned, the sinner will always
escape. The Church may blame; it does not condemn—at most it
does but relegate the sinner to the Mercy of God. The Republic

---

[1] The figure called Albion in *Jerusalem* is said by the best commentators (Messrs. Sloss and Wallis, in the Clarendon Press edition of the
Prophetic Books) to be a symbol of 'the true relation of Time and Space
with Eternity', and so on; and this is no doubt true. But it is also true
that the name stands, as it always has, for England, and this the commentators allow. We do the poem less than justice if we read it, so to
say, 'unpatriotically'; it is a great spiritual appeal to and demand on
England, and the names of the English geography which fill it are not
there by accident. England itself is summoned to be a true relation of
Time and Space with Eternity. I have allowed Blake's possible heresy
on the nature of Justice; it is the more reason for recollecting that that
heresy recalls us to orthodox Love. 'Man is Love' is the maxim, and
no one knew better than Blake what an agony Man finds it.

Forgiveness and Reconciliation

may condemn; it must not blame—the judge has no business to do more than pronounce a sentence. We are not yet—perhaps in this world we shall never be—in that 'state' when the judges themselves may descend to be substitutes for the condemned and to endure in their own persons the sentences they impose. But something like this is already the habit of the Church, for the Church mystically shares the vicarious sufferings of Christ. 'The state of the punisher is eternal death.' In the Church this is so, for in the Church he who takes vengeance is indeed already lost; he is outside the Church, 'outside which is no salvation'; he is outside the City, where as Saint John saw, are dogs and sorcerers and whoremongers, 'and whoever loveth and maketh a lie'. In the Church there is no punishment except when it is invoked and as long as it is invoked; there is no punishment except through and because of pardon. There indeed the holy soul, aware at once of pardon and celestial vengeance, may sigh: 'Both! both!'—too far beyond our vision to be more than momently comprehensible, and only at moments desirable. But it has been declared that the scars of Christ, the wounds of Love, are glorious in heaven; and the justice of God glorifies the scars of Man who is also Love. The alternative?

> *Instead of the Mutual Forgiveness, the Minute Particulars, I see*
> *Pits of bitumen ever burning, artificial riches of the Canaanite*
> *Like Lakes of liquid lead; instead of heavenly Chapels, built*
> *By our dear Lord, I see Worlds crusted with snows and ice.*
> *I see a Wicker Idol woven round Jerusalem's children. I see*
> *The Canaanite, the Amalekite, the Moabite, the Egyptian . . .*
> *Driven on the Void in incoherent despair into Non Entity.*

Blake put the same vision more positively and more simply in one of the shorter poems:

> *Thus through all eternity*
> *I forgive you, you forgive me:*
> *As our dear Redeemer said:*
> *This the Wine and this the Bread.*

The orthodox Christian need not reject that quatrain. If our

181

Lord was indeed the very Person of forgiveness, then certainly it is the very passion of forgiveness which is communicated in the Eucharist; it is a mutuality between God and man which is also expressed between man and man. To feed on that with a grudge or a resentment present in the brain, or still lingering in the blood below the brain, is to reject the divine Food that is swallowed; it is not only to set schism between the body and the soul but literally in the body itself. All things are finally worked out in the body; all mysteries are there manifested, even if still as mysteries. It is the only crucible of the great experiment; its innocent, even if debased, purity endures the most difficult transmutations of the soul.

All this has reference to definite injuries definitely inflicted. But there is more. Since the Fall we have been subjected to pains, illnesses, and distresses whose source is beyond our knowledge. Physical agonies, caused by this and the other physical crisis, afflict us. If these, as has been held, are the result of sin, then they are the result of sinners: sin does not, for us, exist without sinners. But since, for all practical purposes, we do not know those sinners, then, for practical purposes, they do not exist. They may be ancestral or contemporaneous; they may indeed be our ignorant selves. The state of forgiveness must cover these; that is, a reconciliation, a love, must cover them. We must forgive the evils we suffer because of the dreadful co-inherence of all mankind, even if we do not know who inflicts them; and we must be prepared to be forgiven when we discover, knowing wholly and wholly known, the results of our own sin. To dwell on this is superfluous. When we are able to begin to forgive the known, we shall not have very much difficulty in forgiving the unknown; at least there we can believe there was no deliberate malice. True, but there was undeliberate carelessness. There was also our own sinful corruption which certainly infects humanity, somewhere, somehow, with the pain which is its inevitable accompaniment—which is, indeed, its very identity. The whole state of forgiveness must be whole; it is a state of being into which we grow and not a series of acts which we exercise, though (to repeat) we must exercise those acts in faith. Say, Do not do; and add, And then do. The supernatural is the birth of action in the death of action.

> *O point of mutual forgiveness between enemies,*
> *Birthplace of the Lamb of God incomprehensible!*

It was worth remembering Blake. But beyond Blake lies the Lady Julian of Norwich. Few, if any, of the English have written so greatly of pardon as she. She has been quoted already, and it is no part of this book's purpose to rewrite journalistically what she wrote celestially. But on the other hand no one can write a word of the absorption of human activities into that final Glory which the Church declares without remembering his august predecessor; and no book on such a subject ought to close without remembering the final Glory. The Atonement is the name given to an operation; an operation beyond our comprehension, but not beyond our attention; an operation by which everything—even hell—was made a part of that final Glory. The Atonement made possible the forgiveness of sins; or at least made it possible after the best manner. It enabled sin to be fully sin, and it fully counteracted sin. The maniacal obsession of selfishness in which, both necessarily and voluntarily, we live, was nowhere arbitrarily destroyed. I do not say that we do not wish it had pleased God to destroy it; of course, we do, even (many of us) at the small cost of destroying us with it. The penance of our life is too heavy. But in fact he neither forbore to create because we were about to sin nor ceased to sustain when we had begun to sin. It is the choice of a God, not of a man; we should have been less harsh. We should not have created because we could not have endured; we could not have willed; we could not have loved. It is the choice of a God, not of a man.

'This place is prison and this life is penance; and in the remedy he willeth that we rejoice. The remedy is that our Lord is with us, keeping and leading into the fulness of joy.' The joy is to be complete and universal; even (mystically) hell is to be part of that joy. Saint John saw wisely when he saw for a moment the smoke of the torment going up for ever and ever before the Lamb and before his angels, though that is impossible for any of us to understand and live: that is a Glory we cannot and ought not to endure. But at least, whatever 'the smoke of their torment' means, it means something which the glorious company of heaven serenely tolerate, though only the glorious company; we need not be premature. There are things which can only be borne in the farther heavens, as Dante saw when Beatrice refused to smile at him in the nearer because he could not bear the smile. The mystery of unforgiven sin is one of these, and the knowledge of how this also is (if it exists) an element in the eternal joy. It is in every way wiser and better for us to have no part in it here that we may not need to have part in it hereafter. At the very least, if we condemn ourselves to have part in it, we shall have refused for ever the interchange of pardon. Whatever hell is, that interchange by definition it is not.

It is certainly now a part of the mystery to know what the relation may be between those who have been injured and, refusing to forgive, are cut off in hell, and those who have injured and repenting are assumed into heaven. Is it possible to be the occasion, by a committed wrong, of provoking that terrible refusal to forgive, and yet oneself to be in joy? Only the divine reassurance that nothing and no one can be the *cause* of sin except the unrepenting and unforgiving self could be then sufficient to content us. That reassurance will, no doubt, be sufficient; the least movement of Omnipotent Love within. But not to need the reassurance would be better; it would be better not to be compelled to sigh 'O felix culpa' there; better to be, there as here, only the occasion of 'fair love and fear and knowledge and holy hope'. That is not altogether our choice; the avoidance of injuries, nothing else, is. But it will not be better to be known in heaven as a cause of injuries, forgiven or unforgiven, than of none.

Unforgiven sin then is beyond our guess. Forgiven sin, under the Protection, is not; it is forgiven sin that it remains to consider as an element in the Glory. The unusual greatness of the Lady Julian is the two extremes which her book contains on the matter of sin. No one better understood the binding and harrowing nature of sin than she; no one dared a loftier vision of its final transfiguration. What she said of that is contained in the 38th chapter of the *Revelations of Divine Love*. It runs:

'Also God showed that sin shall be no shame to man, but worship. For right as to every sin is answering a pain by truth, right so for every sin, to the same soul is given a bliss by love: right as diverse sins are punished with diverse pains after that they be grievous, right so shall they be rewarded with diverse joys in Heaven after that they have been painful and sorrowful to the soul in earth. For the soul that shall come to Heaven is precious to God, and the place so worshipful that the goodness of God suffereth never that soul to sin that shall come there but which sin shall be rewarded; and it is made known without end, and blissfully restored by overpassing worship.'

'A pain by truth . . . a bliss by love,' 'Man is love.' 'God is Love.' These, in the reverse order—or recurring rather in antiphonal order through the whole spiral of the heavenly stair—are the steps which lead to the knowledge of the new life. All is in the end a question of how we choose to know. Man at the time of the Fall, and continuously and voluntarily since, insisted on knowing good and evil; that is, good *as* evil (since there was nothing but the good to know, the evil could only lie in the manner of knowing). The power had been conceded to him, did he choose to exercise it; he did. There remained but one question of reconciliation: could the evil be wholly known as the means of good?[1] The effect was that man was victim as well as sinner; and if man would know himself as the victim of his own sin—a triumphant or a defiant, but always a sacrificial—victim of sin, then it should be conceded to him to know the endured evil as good: not certainly the original good, for that could not be, but another, a new, good: 'a pain by truth, a bliss by love'.

The Lady's phrase is one that holds the heart and holds it either way. The pain by truth is the exclusion of sin from the City; the bliss by love is the inclusion. In the old Jewish tradition, sin had been secluded into the secret knowledge of God alone. God had been said to have 'forgotten' it: it was no longer

[1] How that was effected is the subject of *The Doctrine of the Atonement* by L. S. Thornton.

to be part of the relationship of the soul with God. It is true that this is still a fact of the spiritual life. 'I must', wrote Kierkegaard, 'have faith that God in forgiving has forgotten what guilt there is . . . in thinking of God I must think that he has forgotten it, and so learn to dare to forget it myself in forgiveness.' That state corresponds to the old Covenant, the Covenant of the simple exterior sacrifice. It is permitted; it is even commanded; we are not to remember our guilt.

Say then, Forget; but add, Do not forget. With the rending of the veil and the entrance of the single High Priest into the state of the Holy of Holies (the perfect re-entry, as it were, into himself), the secluded knowledge was to be shared. In God it was hidden, but then like all things in him it was a hidden joy. With our entry into that renewed knowledge, it was and is to be a joy to us also: a pain by truth, a bliss by love. Forgiveness is the knowing of it so. To call it only remembrance is futile; the act, the sin itself exists in him, as all things exist in him. The exclusion of the sin from himself (were that possible) must unimaginably exist in him. But he would not be content with that, nor would he have us be. That which must be excluded by justice must be included by grace. The sentence in which, more than in most, our most courteous Lord exhibited at once his freedom and his servitude was uttered at the point of the opening of the Holy of Holies. 'Thinkest thou I cannot now pray to my Father, and he shall presently give me more than twelve legions of angels? but how then shall the scriptures be fulfilled, that thus it must be?' Yet the scriptures were only there because he had already decreed that thus it must be. He could—or the Temptation means nothing—have improperly evaded; he could—or his sentence is blasphemy—have properly avoided; but he had decreed that he would do neither. He as Man would forgive *thus*, because men also should not merely be forgiven but also, in every corner of their natures, forgive.

For the Atonement, like many other great, though lesser, resolutions, is physical as well as spiritual—to use once more that fatal intellectual dichotomy which has done so much harm to Christendom. It is, say rather, carried out in the blood as well as the soul; the final seal of all things in this creation of our Lord God's is physical; it was, as was said at the beginning, his very purpose in it. The forgiveness of sins, therefore, is a physical thing; that it certainly must be so before it is fully operative in every way is shown by the many times when the best intentions of our minds are overthrown by the revolt of our nerves. They are probably not as many as those when our minds quite steadily decline, in spite often of the witness of the flesh, to forgive or to ensure forgiveness. The flesh continually testifies, after its own manner, to the good. Our bodies are innocent compared to our souls, and their guiltiness is but that which they are compelled to borrow from the fallen will.

'By the fall', wrote William Law, 'of our first father we have lost our first glorious bodies, that eternal, celestial flesh and blood which had as truly the nature of paradise and Heaven in it as our present bodies have the nature, mortality and corruption of this world in them: if, therefore, we are to be redeemed there is an absolute necessity that our souls be clothed again with this first paradisaical or heavenly flesh and blood, or we can never enter into the Kingdom of God. Now this is the reason why the Scriptures speak so particularly, so frequently, and so emphatically of the powerful blood of Christ, of the great benefit it is to us, of its redeeming, quickening, life-giving virtue; it is because our first life or heavenly flesh and blood is born again in us, or derived again into us from this blood of Christ.

'Our blessed Lord, who died for us, had not only that outward flesh and blood, which He received from the Virgin Mary, and which died upon the Cross, but He had also a holy humanity of heavenly flesh and blood veiled under it, which was appointed by God to quicken, generate, and bring forth from itself such a holy offspring of immortal flesh and blood as Adam the first should have brought forth before his fall.'

It was this heavenly humanity which forgave; say, he forgave in his flesh, and therefore his very flesh forgave. As God, he could, no doubt, have forgiven—it is but to repeat from another angle what was said just now; all the masters of that doctrine sound it together; what without the Incarnation he could not have done—what, had he (*per impossibile*) after the Fall rejected the Incarnation, he could not have done—would have been to forgive as Man. 'When Adam fell, God's Son fell'—not in the sense of sin but of distress—'because of the rightful one-ing which had been made in heaven God's Son might not be disparted from Adam. For by Adam I understand All-Man.' It is therefore that the Eucharist is also that forgiveness of his flesh, and that we literally feed on forgiveness. Otherwise our now so-charged bodies would not have laboured with that vocation which, more than we suppose, is their own, however exacerbated they are with it. They are sometimes in revolt because our bodies are physically aware of the co-inherence with other bodies which our mental pickings and choosings reject. For—to quote the Lady Julian again—'Kind'—that is, Nature—'and Grace are of one accord: for Grace is of God, as Kind is of God: he is two in manner of working and one in love; and neither of these worketh without other: nor may they be disparted'.

What has blame outside the Glory of God has worship within the Glory, provided that the blame can bring itself to come into the Glory. In the *Paradiso* of Dante a similar doctrine is laid down. In the third heaven Cunizza di Romano says to him 'Joyously now do I grant indulgence to myself for the occasion of my fate here'; that is, she blessedly pardons herself for her being no higher or holier in heaven, taking delight in God's will; for in heaven 'joy brings brightness'; and a few lines later the soul of Folco of Marseilles says the same thing: 'Here we do not repent; we smile; not at the sin which does not come again to mind, but at the Worth that orders and provides . . . the Good which turns the world below into that which is above.' Beyond that sphere, Dante says in a tremendous metaphor, colour ceases; the redeemed spirits are seen by their light alone.

That extreme effort to express the lofty (but not unfleshed) diagram of redemption should not detain us too long. Its value to us is that it restores us again to facts and not to what we feel about facts: it is to acts that we must return, for it is in acts that the Glory of God exists among us. It is permitted to us to be its occasions, but mostly here by faith. The splendour of it is not always obvious, nor the brightness of the joy. It is, again, permitted to us to encourage the joy; it is indeed commanded. But though the command is primary in itself, it is secondary in relation to the other commanded virtues. Chastity is before it, and truthfulness (that is, accuracy), and industry, and the duties of magnificence; and love, and therefore forgiveness. It is better to know it in joy, but it is still more important to know it, forgiving or forgiven. Either way there are depths within depths. For a proper forgiveness is so full a matter of the spirit that it leads to the very centre of the Union. It is an exchange of hearts. To forgive another involves, sooner or later, so full an understanding of the injury, and of its cause, that in some sense we ourselves have committed the injury; we are that which injures ourselves. And to be this we must very greatly have got out of ourselves; and this is the means and seal of the Church. The Church consists only of those who have so gone out of themselves or are going or desire to go out of themselves. The little word 'as' in the Lord's Prayer is the measurement of the distance gone. Its final reach is to the Union; the inGodding of man.

It is in relation to the inGodding that the clause in the Apostles' Creed stands as one of the definitions of eternity. The last paragraph is almost a description of the heavenly City of the Apocalypse. 'I believe in the Holy Ghost' is the foundation; 'the Holy Catholic Church' is the streets and markets, the great co-inherence of souls; 'the Communion of Saints, the Forgiveness of Sins, the Resurrection of the Body and the Life Everlasting' are the four enclosing walls; and yet that metaphor is too remote, for all are but four titles for the same co-inherence of relationship. The Communion of Saints involves the resurrection of all the past, and therefore the forgiveness of sins. The resurrection involves forgiveness and communion. But the forgiveness is the necessity of all. Where love is fate, this is fate.

CHAPTER VIII

The Present Time

There lies now[1] in many minds the general consideration of our relation to our present enemies. This problem, for those who feel it, is involved, of course, in all the preceding pages; it has here and there been specifically alluded to. I do not feel myself in the best position to press it further, since, except for that inconvenience, loss, separation, and distress in which we are all involved, I have not so far suffered any direct disaster on account of the war; that is, on account of my country's enemies. What I have suffered I might easily have suffered anyhow. Just as every death which is now died too soon must have been died in the end, and could not then be avoided, so our present unhappiness might for any and each of us have come had there been no war, or something very much like it. We do not avoid misery by avoiding *this* misery; it is always the present misery which is unbearable, and existence, but for that, might, we feel, have been almost happy. It is false; our suffering

is permanent, obscure, and dark
and hath the nature of infinity.

And our enemies, or the great majority of them, know it as well as we.

To press guilt upon them therefore is, to begin with, unwise; we are all caught in the same trap. To begin therefore to forgive the present German Government or indeed the Germans for our financial loss or our personal separation is for most of us nonsense; it is as difficult to forgive as to indict a nation. Without a direct sense of present personal injury by a particular person or persons there can hardly be any question of forgiveness.

[1] This was written in 1942.

But, it will be said, there are those who have directly suffered. There is also the sense of offence against morals—the treaty-breaking and the massacres. It is presumably the thought of those two problems which causes Mr. Churchill to refer to Herr Hitler as 'that bad man'. One must distinguish between the rhetorical force of the phrase and its literal meaning. The rhetorical force is of the greatest value to us at the present time, and may, of course, be entirely justified. It comes to us with a sense of the greatest sincerity, but that is only to say that Mr. Churchill is a superb rhetorician. In view of human history one can hardly believe that rhetoric necessarily implies sincerity. Men may be greatly moved by liars and knaves; indeed, we ourselves or many of us tend to assert that the Germans and Italians have precisely allowed themselves to be moved by liars and knaves. Our confidence in the Prime Minister need not be based on his style of public abuse. But the phrase 'that bad man' does sum up a very general belief among the English people, Christians and non-Christians alike.

(1) To take the first problem first. It is clear that most of us cannot and ought not to start to forgive Herr Hitler on behalf of others. I say Herr Hitler for convenience of discussion, but the discussion applies equally to the German Government, or the Nazi party, or indeed the whole German people, so far as they are not covered by the modifications proposed in the first paragraph of this section. It is our enemies we are concerned with; to say our enemy singularly intensifies but does not alter the discussion; so long, at any rate, as we continue to regard Herr Hitler as a responsible human being. If we prefer to think him mad, we cannot hold him as responsible, and the discussion ceases. You cannot forgive a madman for you cannot be in proper rational relation with him. You can, I suppose, love him by such an act of goodwill as one might exercise towards a cat or an angel. But his life (as Wordsworth said) 'is hid with Christ in God'; it is alien from us. There can be no mutuality.

One cannot then forgive on behalf of others. The fact that many of us resent injuries on behalf of others is generally a convenient way of indulging our resentments with an appearance of

justice. Not always, certainly; there is such a thing as holy anger
—'the golden blazonries of Love irate'—mingled with compassion. But holy anger is a very dangerous thing indeed for any
who are not saints to play about with; and I am not clear that it
is very often found in the saints. Supernatural indignation springs
from a supernatural root; our business generally is to look to the
root. But if a facile resentment on behalf of others is unwise, so
is a facile pardon; and other than a facile pardon is a very deep
matter. I am not saying that it is impossible. It is to be admitted
that a man profoundly and permanently injured by a particular
German—say, a man who had been deliberately crippled or a
woman who had seen her husband tortured—might feel himself
unable to reach that state of forgiveness which he conceived to be
his duty. He might therefore entreat anyone who loved him to
make an effort in that direction on his behalf. Much may be done
by a vicarious virtue, so only that the original desire remains
sincere and industrious. A man may begin to be generous or
devout or even chaste in and through another, so long as his own
efforts to join himself with that virtue do not fail. This certainly
is the ground of our moral union with Christ, but that union may
itself be mediated from him through others. This is part of the
work of the great contemplative Orders; the invocation of saints
is the union of heaven and earth in the same labour; on earth the
vision of romantic love is a vision of virtue in another, and by the
union of his devotion with this a lover begins to follow the Way.
There are circles who are pledged to the consideration of these
mysteries, the exchange and union of intentions. But such a
vicarious beauty of achievement in forgiveness is a very different
thing from the lamentable folly of those who hurry, unharmed,
to forgive or not to forgive harm done to others. It is the direct
purpose of the injured alone that matters.

This attempt at direct forgiveness then means, as has been
said before, whether towards Herr Hitler or the lowest creature
in the Gestapo, an attempt at direct goodwill, at the recollection
and the knowledge of the injury in love. It will be very hard; it
will also be very dull. Forgiveness is not normally a thrilling or
an exciting thing. The metaphor which our Lord used has a par-

ticular aptness—it is the taking up, the carrying, the Cross, not the being crucified; it is the intolerable *weight* of the duty, and not its agony, which defeats us—'the *weight* of glory'. We do not (perhaps we need not) generally get as far as the Crucifixion. The direct injury, however lasting, is not to be allowed to deflect attention from doing the best thing at the moment; the best thing, that is, for the Church, and therefore best for our enemy and best for ourselves. The best for the Church means the best in Christ. The conversion, where it is demanded, of the wild justice of revenge to the civil justice of the Divine City is the precise operation of the Holy Spirit towards Christ. All we need to do is to attend to the goodwill, to the civility; the justice (in the personal relation) can be left to Christ. 'Vengeance is mine; I will repay, saith the Lord.' It is perhaps desirable to notice that the repayment is not limited to our enemy. We shall be unfortunate if we forget the trespasses, the debts, which our enemies desire to repay with their wild justice and are content to leave to his promise. It is important that we should be ready to forgive the Germans; it is not unimportant to recognize that many Germans (including Herr Hitler? possibly; we do not very well know) may feel that they have much to forgive us. Many reconciliations have unfortunately broken down because both parties have come prepared to forgive and unprepared to be forgiven. Instruction is as badly needed in this as in many other less vital things; that holy light which we call humility has an exact power of illumination all its own.

(2) The problem of the general moral law is more difficult to define and not much more easy to practise. It was alluded to in Chapter VI, but what was said there may perhaps be repeated. There is in existence at the present time, so far as I know, no penal code of international law. There are, that is to say, no announced penalties, in the name of international law, against national offenders. There are, of course, the sanctions of the League of Nations; but they were intended rather to discourage than to punish, and they were intended to cease when they had served their purpose of preventing or defeating aggression. There is no legal way by which a breaker of treaties can be

brought before a tribunal; there is indeed no tribunal for him to be brought before. We have not been able to establish one because none of the nations have found themselves able to trust the capacity of other nations for just decision; there is no need to look for worse motives; and indeed, considering humanity, such a hesitation might be thought simple caution. But that being so, there is, so far as I can see, no way of punishing an offender, nor therefore any method of formal acquittal or pardon. The experience of the Versailles Treaty (not that I wish to attack it as a whole) in which the Germans were compelled to admit their guilt in 1914, was not encouraging, nor, obviously, can be. It is (when all modifications have been made) too much like confessions extracted under torture. It would be conceivable, since murder is regarded as a criminal offence in all States, to declare that it is a criminal offence as between States, and that the beginning of military operations without declaration of war, or the destruction of Rotterdam, were murder. It would be possible to set up a tribunal to declare this, and then to bring prisoners before it. But it would be a retrospective decision, and some things (for example, the English bombing of German civilians— however justified or not) would put the tribunal in an ugly light. It would be, in the end, only a regularized and formal vengeance. We can take vengeance if we choose, but we must call it vengeance, for to take blood for blood without the specific contractual agreement of preordained law is precisely vengeance.

There is certainly a sense in which execution might be done; we might turn vengeance into sacrifice. It is dangerous, but it could be done. It puts almost too high—perhaps entirely too high—a responsibility on mortal men, but it is a responsibility we could accept if we chose. It might be declared that, though we had no precedent, we intended to establish a precedent. The new League of Nations (whatever form it may take) should not only rise out of the blood that has been shed in the war; it should be definitely dedicated to the future with blood formally shed. If we are indeed victorious, and if our chief enemies fell into our hands, we might begin a new habit among the nations. We could not pretend we had any justification for it; it would be a new thing.

We should say, in effect: 'We have no right to punish you for what you have done in the past. We admit it entirely. But we are determined that we will make it dangerous for men to do as you have done; we will make it a matter of death. We shall sacrifice you to that new thing, though because it has not yet existed you cannot be guilty under it and must therefore be innocent of it. We shall therefore sacrifice you to our intentions; and so awful a thing is this that it is an example, and the only worthy example, of how mighty a thing we are trying to do.'

> *This shall make*
> *Our purpose necessary and not envious,*
> *Which so appearing to the common eyes*
> *We shall be called purgers, not murderers.*

But the purgation would be of our own hearts. The execution of our enemy after that manner would be an admission of our solidarity with him. We should execute him not because he was different from us, but because we were the same as he. The shedding of that blood would be a pronunciation of a sentence against us and our children if we denied or disobeyed the law we had newly made. It would be an offering, by the co-inherence of man, of the blood of the co-inherence. 'It is good', said Caiaphas, and spoke a truth all civil governments have been compelled to maintain—and ecclesiastical also; why else were heretics condemned? —'that one man should die for the people.' But then, humanly, the people must know their blood one with his; they can only thrive by his if they are willing that their own should be shed; and they must know that so, but only so, they do thrive by his. They must, in fact, answer, according to their degree: 'His blood be on us and on our children.'

It may be held—the question must be left to the theologians—that this is impossible for Christians. It would perhaps be too like a pagan sacrifice, too much like Hiel who built up Jericho—'he laid the foundation thereof in Abiram his firstborn, and set up the gates thereof in his youngest son Segub', or like the fable of Agamemnon who sacrificed his daughter Iphigenia at the bidding of a god. It is said that she was caught away in a cloud as

The Forgiveness of Sins

Isaac was saved by the interposition of a ram—the God of Israel maintained always (and in the end at his own expense) the atonement of blood. But whatever the result, whether the God was pitiful and forbore, or exact and accepted, or redeeming and substituted; whether Iphigenia was saved, or Abiram and Segub died, or Isaac was exchanged, yet human sacrifice has been forbidden to the new law, and by sacrifice is meant the dedicated ritual offering. To lose a thing by death or otherwise, even to kill a thing, is not necessarily to sacrifice it; the word is used too cheaply. It would have been supposed, not long ago, that human sacrifice as such, so ritual and dedicated, would have been impossible to our civilization, but so much has returned that this too might return. Indeed, the only difference between this and the sacrifice of our enemy discussed above, is that whereas this is to a God, that is only to our best substitute for a God—our own solemn purposes for the future. Even so, it is greater than mere vengeance; it involves, for good or for evil, greater dreams of power. It is true that many people would be shocked at the thought of sacrifice who are not at all shocked at the idea of vengeance. They are perhaps right (or at least they would be if they had any idea of what they were thinking and saying). The problem is like that other—of adultery and divorce. Adultery is bad morals, but divorce is bad metaphysics. Bloody vengeance is a sin, but the bloody sacrifice is outrage.

It is, therefore, even for our future, our intention, our safety (could it ensure them), forbidden to the Church. Whether it is conceded outside the Church is another matter; the Church, refusing it in one sense, may allow it in another, as she does with divorce. But she herself must not tamper with it. Those who sincerely reject the Single Sacrifice may perhaps be driven back on the many types of it, even if—no, because the centrality of all the types is unacknowledged. But belief in the Single must refuse the multiplicity. The Rite of the shedding of blood for atonement or for achievement is accomplished. No other shedding of that kind is allowed, unless God permits and enforces by physical states or spiritual or both. Women's periods present the one; the death of martyrs the other; the Eucharist both. War and capital punishment are retained by the Republic, and the Church concedes them to the Republic—on the understanding that they are invoked only by the guilty. His guilt is the invocation. 'A just war' means that the unjust party invokes blood; it is his due, and he shall have it; the unatoning blood. But the theologians must decide.

It seems then that there are, as regards our enemy, four possibilities, both in the temper of our spirit now and afterwards, and in action afterwards: vengeance, justice, sacrifice, and forgiveness. Of these, vengeance is in fact as difficult as any other, for it is bound to be a limited vengeance, and that is always a disappointing as well as an evil thing. It is not, I suppose, intended to put all Germans (or even a majority) to death, and if not then whoever demands full vengeance will be disappointed. They will have encouraged themselves to hate the survivors, as the survivors will certainly hate them. It is sometimes held that only by such a 'lesson'—that is, by the teaching of such doctrine—can our enemies be taught. This book is not the place to discuss it, nor should be. In so far as the idea of vengeance enters, it is forbidden to the Christian to participate, mentally or physically.

(2) Justice, in any legal sense, is impossible, for there is no legal sense. 'The eye for an eye' principle takes us straight back into vengeance; any other principle of penal justice demands prestatement, and it has not been stated. The enactment of retrospective international law would again take us into vengeance (as a state of mind) or else into sacrifice. That would depend on the state of mind, but either way justice is impossible.[1]

(3) Sacrifice is possible to the non-Christian; it may be forbidden to the Christian. Even for the non-Christian it depends on an integrity of purpose, on a depth of co-inherence, almost im-

---

[1] I do not wish to seem to rule out such things as the immediate occupation or disarmament of the enemy countries, or the immediate display there of military power and the formal result of defeat in war. There is a difference between the immediate control of an attack and the decision on future relations. It is, however, a dangerous period; extension of control, as we all know in many other and less widespread cases, always has everything diplomatic, and generally has nothing decent, to be said for it.

The Forgiveness of Sins

possible to be understood. To kill' the rulers of Germany, to destroy Germany, is a vicarious action; that is to say, unless it is sacrifice it is murder, and if it is sacrifice, it is sacrifice, to God or man, on our behalf. The blood is shed on behalf of our purpose and our life, and the lives and purposes of our children; if we betray those purposes we become guilty of the blood; it becomes murder. It is a kind of image in human terms of the Sacrifice in Christian; since there can now be no other deliberate image of that blood to Christians, that sacrifice is forbidden to Christians.

Vengeance then is forbidden; sacrifice is forbidden; justice is impossible: what remains? the fourth choice? forgiveness? and how then forgiveness?

It has been claimed here that forgiveness is a mutual act, but a disposition towards forgiveness is a necessary preliminary towards that act. The mutual act depends on two (or more) single dispositions; we are not excused from our disposition because our enemies refuse to participate, nor is theirs less holy because we will not admit it. He who will claim the supernatural must claim it wholly; its validity cannot be divided; like the Blessed Trinity Itself it lives according to its proper complex method, but it altogether lives as a unity; what we call the natural is but a part of the whole method. The mutual act of forgiveness is a holy thing; the proper dispositions towards it, accepted or not accepted, remain holy. Who decides whether those dispositions are proper? whether repentance is indeed repentance, or whether it is fear or greed or hate masquerading as repentance? must we? In fact we do because we must. No doubt in the end only God knows all, and we may forgive a hypocrite or reject a penitent. The danger of the last is the greater; because our enemy may be penitent? no, but because we ought to be. It is (let it be repeated) the guilty who forgives and not the innocent; not perhaps the guilty in that one act, but guilty of how much else, of how much that led up to that act, guilty even in the very act of mutual pardon—that is, of mutual reconciled love—of how much of weakness, folly, reluctance, pride, or greed. The guilty repents; the as greatly guilty forgives; there is therefore but one maxim for both: 'make haste'. It is one thing to be reasonably intelligent, but quite another to be curiously inquisitive or carefully watchful. We are part of him and he of us; that is the centre; by his death there—his death in that repentance—we live and he by ours: 'dying each other's life, living each other's death'. It is all a question of whether he and we choose or do not choose.

Both must wish, and will, to be a part of an act. Do, and do not do. The union is in us becoming a part of the act, not in the act being a part of us. But if one of us does not wish to be? if we refuse co-inherence? 'Ephraim is joined to idols; let him alone.' If a man will be separate from the love which is man's substance, he can; the ancient promise holds: 'I will choose their delusions.' We had better be very sure indeed that we have been injured at the heart before we even think about forgiving; we had better be very careful indeed that we are not forgiving others' injuries, or no injuries, or merely the inevitable pain of existence. Even our enemy is not the universe, and we had better take care to forgive him as himself (if we must) and not the universe in him. But then we may pray to be in our degree made a part of that act which is God and he and we—the act we have only to be.

Whoever refuses . . . it is difficult to see what else can be done except to leave him alone. If he shuts himself out of the mortal co-inherence, or we; if he shuts himself out of the act in which, more than any other, the mortal co-inheres with the divine, or we; then that solitude is the answer. If it is he who refuses, and we have been sincere in our goodwill, then at least we are innocent there—if we have not supposed ourselves to be innocent in anything else. It is on the readiness and the speed with which we move to become part of that act that all depends; so, corrupt, we may put on incorruption, and, mortal, immortality. The reason why a thing possible between men and women individually is almost impossible communally is, obviously, that communities are not individuals; the analogy fails. There are bound to be the innocent among the guilty there; there are misunderstandings which cannot be explained, helplessnesses which ought not, on any plea of justice or for any kind of claim, to be injured.

It is a lame conclusion? a very lame conclusion. Mortal ones are apt to be; only divine conclusions conclude. That the divine conclusion, being timeless, 'entered time' at a particular moment in time does not seem to help much. The weight of glory is the weight of the carrying the cross, 'customary life's exceeding injocundity'. The labour towards our enemy, individual or national, is a continual duty—all Christians say so. Christian publicists indeed, in that as in so many other things, are apt to sound as if they thought they performed their moral duty merely by teaching it; it is easier to write a book repeating that God is love than to think it; it is easier, that is, to say it publicly than to think it privately. Unfortunately, to be of any use, it has to be thought very privately, and thought very hard. To be used towards that thought is, after trying to think it ourselves, our chief business. It is the thought of the world which matters, but thought, like charity, begins at home. It has indeed been held that thought and charity were one; certainly charity is not so much a colour of thought as a particular kind of thought. I had almost said, of accurate thought, but then there is no other. Charity is not a delay in our usual mental habits; it is a change of mental habit; it is the restoration of accurate mental habit. This is everyone's business, for his friend's sake and his enemy's and his own. And if indeed we are all in danger of hell, then very much for his own.

CPSIA information can be obtained at www.ICGtesting.com
Printed in the USA
LVOW10s2026270815

451798LV00001B/76/P